# Sage Accounts

# Made Simple

## Second Edition

# Sage Accounts
# Made Simple
## Second Edition

P.K.McBride

**MADE SIMPLE**
**BOOKS**

OXFORD   AMSTERDAM   BOSTON   LONDON   NEW YORK   PARIS
SAN DIEGO   SAN FRANCISCO   SINGAPORE   SYDNEY   TOKYO

Made Simple is an imprint of Elsevier
Linacre House, Jordan Hill, Oxford OX2 8DP, UK
30 Corporate Drive, Suite 400, Burlington, MA 01803, USA

First edition 1998
Second edition 2002
Reprinted 2003, 2004, 2005, 2006, 2007

**British Library Cataloguing in Publication Data**
A catalogue record for this book is available from the British Library

**Library of Congress Cataloging-in-Publication Data**
A catalog record for this book is available from the Library of Congress

ISBN: 978-0-7506-5810-2

For information on all Made Simple publications
visit our website at http://books.elsevier.com

Printed and bound in *Great Britain*

07 08 09 10  10 9 8 7 6

Working together to grow
libraries in developing countries

www.elsevier.com | www.bookaid.org | www.sabre.org

ELSEVIER   BOOK AID
International   Sabre Foundation

# Contents

# Preface

Sage is the leading producer of accountancy software. Its applications are used in businesses large and small throughout much of the world – and the software will grow with you as you progress from a small to a large business! The current product range includes Instant Accounting, Line 50, Line 100 and other 'Lines' for even larger networks, with variations within each level. All Sage systems have the same core routines and file formats, but the Line systems have network capability, and the higher-specification variations in all ranges have additional modules providing more sophisticated financial control facilities. This book is based on the common core.

Sage software has been so successful because it is designed with business people, not computer people, in mind. The clear layouts, logical structures and thorough error-trapping routines make the applications quick to learn and easy to use.

Sage accounting systems are based on the standard three ledgers (Sales, Purchase, Nominal) and double-entry system of bookkeeping. If you are already using this system for your accounts, then the transition from manual bookkeeping to computerised accounts will be simple and straightforward – start reading this book at Chapter 2. If you have previously been using a cash book, a single ledger system or have simply put everything into a shoebox and handed it to the accountant at the end of the year, then Chapter 1 is for you. It outlines those basic concepts that you should understand before you start to use the software.

# 1 Principles of accounts

# The common basis

Though businesses vary enormously in what they do and how they do it, large parts of their accounting systems are essentially the same. An electrician, a violin-maker, a Web design partnership, a clothes manufacturer, a chain store and the chap who runs the corner-shop may not seem to have much in common. They deal in different products and services; some employ many people, others work alone; some have many – anonymous – customers, some work for a few carefully-cultivated clients; some deal almost entirely in cash, others trade on credit with their customers and suppliers. Despite this, basic structures and operations of their accounts are the same.

Every business has:

♦ **Customers** to whom they supply goods or services.

♦ **Suppliers** of goods and services – from accountancy to Yellow Pages ads. A manufacturing business will also have suppliers of raw materials.

♦ **Owner(s)** – a sole trader, a group of partners or the shareholders of a company.

♦ **Assets** – premises, vehicles, machinery, office furniture and equipment.

The business may also have **employees**. The standard Sage accounts software handles wages, tax and National Insurance as business expenses, but does not cover individual employees' work records and wage slips. A Payroll module is available if required.

## Why keep accounts?

❑ So that the business's owners and backers can see that it is being run honestly by its managers and other employees.

❑ To monitor the business's progress and anticipate – and prevent – problems.

❑ The tax men – and Companies House, for limited companies – get very upset if you don't!

# The common structure

... and the flow of money, goods and services between the components.

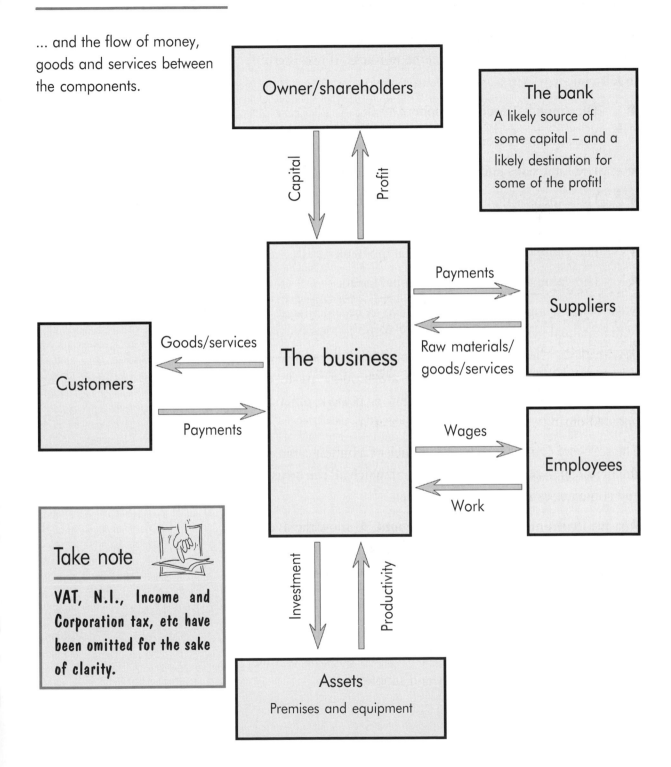

Owner/shareholders

Capital

Profit

**The bank**
A likely source of some capital – and a likely destination for some of the profit!

The business

Payments

Suppliers

Raw materials/ goods/services

Goods/services

Customers

Payments

Wages

Employees

Work

Investment

Productivity

**Take note**

VAT, N.I., Income and Corporation tax, etc have been omitted for the sake of clarity.

Assets

Premises and equipment

3

# Accounts and information

The purpose of any accounting system is to record transactions and to provide information about the business. It must be able to tell you:

◇ The amounts owed to suppliers.

◇ The amounts owed to you by customers.

◇ The total sales and purchases during a period.

◇ The expenses incurred in running the business, e.g. rent, power, stationery, salaries.

◇ The value of cash in hand and at the bank.

◇ The value of the business's capital assets.

Most of these amounts and values have to be calculated, and with a manual system, that takes time. With the Sage systems, as with all good accounts software, the calculations are done for you. Most of the totals and values are brought up to date automatically as each new transaction is posted; others are updated during end-of-year routines.

The software can also produce, at a click of a button, a range of financial statements and summaries – of which all can be useful and some are essential. These include:

◇ A **Profit and Loss (P&L) Account**, to show the overall trading position. Is the business making a profit? And how much?

◇ A **Balance Sheet**, showing the assets and liabilities.

◇ **Departmental analyses** of profit and loss.

◇ **Summaries** and **graphs** showing the patterns of trade with individual customers and suppliers.

◇ **VAT returns**.

# Double-entry bookkeeping

## Jargon

- ❑ Account: a record of the transactions relating to one aspect of the business's dealings

- ❑ Debit: movement of value into an account – e.g. goods that have been purchased, or the income from sales.

- ❑ Credit: movement of value out of an account, e.g. the money to pay for purchases.

- ❑ Posting: recording transactions in the accounts.

Double-entry bookkeeping is the basis of all modern accounting systems. It works like this.

A separate account – record of transactions – is kept for each customer and supplier, for each category of expenses, assets and debts, for each bank account, etc.

## Debit and credit

It is double-entry bookkeeping because every transaction is recorded twice – as a *debit* in one account and as a *credit* in another. When an item is purchased, its value is added to the appropriate expense or stock account (debit), and the same amount removed from a cash or bank account (credit).

| Purchases Account | | | |
|---|---|---|---|
| Debit | £ | Credit | £ |
| 300 widgets (bank) | 690 | | |

| Bank Account | | | |
|---|---|---|---|
| Debit | £ | Credit | £ |
| | | Purchases | 690 |

Because the movement of money into one account is always balanced by an outward movement from another, the totals of the credits and debits should always be the same. A Trial Balance (page 11), which compares those totals, provides a first-level check of the accuracy of the accounts.

# Assets and liabilities

An **asset** is something which we own, or is owed to us – something which can be turned into cash. Assets are divided into two categories:

♦ **Fixed assets**: those of more or less constant value, such buildings, equipment, furnishings and vehicles.

♦ **Current assets**: those which fluctuate during trading, such as stock, cash in the bank and monies owed by customers.

Assets are recorded as debit entries when they are acquired, with balancing credit entries – mainly in the bank account.

**Liabilities** are the amounts owed by the business. They are also divided into two categories:

♦ **Current liabilities**: debts which change during trading – money owed in taxes or to suppliers, bank overdrafts.

♦ **'Financed By'**: the heading normally used to cover share capital, bank loans and other long-term debts.

# Capital

The term is used loosely to mean several slightly different things. When a business is first started, *capital* refers to the money put into it to get things going. A loan is sometimes referred to as *working capital*, though strictly speaking this means the difference between current assets and current liabilities.

In an on-going business, capital can be defined as the excess of assets over liabilities – the value of the business if all its assets are sold and debts paid.

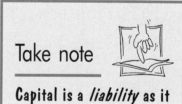

**Take note**

Capital is a *liability* as it is the money owed by the business to its owners.

# Example: The start-up

Smith and Jones pool their savings to start a business. Their first moves are to buy a machine to make widgets, and a van to deliver them. Here are the key accounts after the initial set up.

These accounts are hugely simplified! Transactions would normally be recorded in far more detail – at the very least they should have the date and an invoice or other reference number. There should a clear 'audit trail', making it simple to trace the flow of money through the business.

Each account has been totalled to give its current balance. Add up debit and credit balances and you get the same £20,000 total.

## Capital Account

| Debit | £ | Credit | £ |
|---|---|---|---|
| | | Smith (Bank) | 10,000 |
| | | Jones (Bank) | 10,000 |
| | | Balance | 20,000 |

## Vehicles Account

| Debit | £ | Credit | £ |
|---|---|---|---|
| Van (Bank) | 8,000 | | |
| Balance | 8,000 | | |

## Equipment Account

| Debit | £ | Credit | £ |
|---|---|---|---|
| Machine (Bank) | 4,000 | | |
| Balance | 4,000 | | |

## Bank Account

| Debit | £ | Credit | £ |
|---|---|---|---|
| Smith (Capital) | 10,000 | | |
| Jones (Capital) | 10,000 | | |
| | 20,000 | Van (Vehicles) | 8,000 |
| | | Machine (Equip't) | 4,000 |
| | | | 12,000 |
| Balance | | | |
| 20,000 - 12,000 = | 8,000 | | |

# Customers and suppliers

In a paper-based system, the individual accounts are held in *books of account*, or *ledgers* – the *Sales*, *Purchases* and *Nominal Ledgers*. The Sage system follows this convention, but calls them *Customers*, *Suppliers* and *Nominal*.

## The Sales Ledger (Customers)

If customers buy from you on credit, they will each have their own separate account, where you record the date and value of each sale and of payment made. With Sage software, not only can you easily see which payments are outstanding – and for how long – you can just as easily generate reminder letters to the slower-paying debtors. There is also a **Graph** facility which can give you a good overview of your trading with any selected customer.

The Sales Ledger is a collection of customers' accounts. There will be one or more other accounts – in the Nominal Ledger – which keep track of sales overall. A small firm might just have one general Sales account; a larger one is more likely to have Sales accounts for each area of the firm's business.

## The Purchase Ledger (Suppliers)

This is the mirror image of the Sales Ledger, recording the details of your dealings – on credit – with your suppliers. Each entry will be matched by a balancing entry in the Nominal Ledger, where there will be accounts for purchases of stock and raw materials, and other expenses.

- ❑ Debtors: those who owe you money.

- ❑ Creditors: those to whom the business owes money.

- ❑ Purchases: refers only to raw materials and goods bought for resale. All other costs are expenses.

Tip

**Cash sales can be recorded directly into the Sales and Bank accounts. It may be worth using Customer accounts for immediate payers if you want to monitor your trade with them.**

# The Nominal Ledger

## Take note

If your transactions are all cash (i.e. paid more or less immediately) you only need Nominal ledger accounts. All transaction can be recorded through the Bank routines (Chapter 7).

This is the heart of the system – indeed, if you have no credit sales or purchases, it is the only one you need. All accounts, except those for individual credit customers and suppliers, are stored here.

Exactly how you organise your Nominal accounts is up to you – they should reflect the realities of your business. As a general rule, you set up an account for each aspect of the money flow that you want to be able to monitor. For example, in a small business, where the office expenses only add up to a few hundred a year, one account would be adequate to record them all. In a larger firm, separate accounts for paper, postage, cleaning, electricity, coffee, etc. would enable managers to see clearly how and when money was being spent – and therefore to forecast future spending, and perhaps find some savings.

Some accounts are essential. You must have ones for:

♦ Capital and long-term loans

♦ Fixed assets

♦ Cash in hand and at the bank

♦ Sales of goods and services

♦ Expenses.

A retailing or manufacturing business would also need accounts for:

♦ Purchases of goods and materials, and current stock

♦ Labour, advertising and other expenses directly related to producing and selling your goods.

If the firm trades on credit with its customers and suppliers it will also need accounts for its creditors and debtors.

# The Nominal Ledger in Sage

When you first set up Sage accounts, the wizard creates a comprehensive set of Nominal accounts. These vary slightly, depending upon the nature of your business, and we will look later (page 50) at how to adapt or add to them further, for the moment just notice the way they are organised.

Each account has a reference number, or *Nominal Code*, and they are numbered so that similar ones are close together. When summaries are being prepared, related accounts can be totalled by setting ranges. For example, the first four accounts are:

      0010   Freehold Property

      0011   Leasehold Property

      0012   Land

      0020   Plant and Machinery

The total of the range 0010 to 0012 is the value of all property and land. If you wanted to create accounts for more categories of property or land, by numbering them 0013, 0014, etc, you only need to extend the range to get a summary property value.

A little further down the list you will find

      0030   Office Equipment

      0040   Furniture and Fixtures

      0050   Motor Vehicles

Setting the range 0010 to 0050 will therefore give the value of all fixed assets.

This pattern runs right through the system, with groups of related accounts separated from the next by breaks in the number sequence. An outline of the structure is shown here on the right.

# The Nominal structure

Fixed assets
0 –      Premises, etc
Current Assets
1000 –  Stock
1100 –  Debtors
1200 –  Bank
Current Liabilities
2100 –  Creditors
2200 –  Tax Control
2300 –  Loans
Capital & Reserves
3000 –  Share capital
3200 –  Profit & Loss
Sales/Income
4000 –  Sales/work done
4200 –  Sales of assets
4900 –  Other sales/income
Purchases
5000 –  Materials
5200 –  Stock
Direct Expenses
6000 –  Labour
6200 –  Advertising
Overheads
7000 –  Wages & Salaries
7100 –  Premises costs
7200 –  Expenses
8000 –  Depreciation
Trouble-shooting
9998 –  Suspense A/c
9999 –  Mispostings

# The Trial Balance

The Trial Balance show the current debit and credit balance on each account, and the total of all debits and credits.

In a manual system, it is used to check that data has been (double-)entered correctly – the sum of the debit and credit balances should be equal. If they are not, it shows that with at least one transaction one or both of the values has been entered wrongly or in the wrong column, or has been omitted altogether.

In a Sage system this cannot happen as the value entered for a transaction is automatically posted to two accounts – once as a debit and once as a credit. A discrepancy here would show that the data had become corrupted.

G.A. Jones T/A PlumbCrazy
Trial Balance

| N/C | Name | Debit | Credit |
|---|---|---|---|
| 0020 | Plant and Machinery | 5,000.00 | |
| 0030 | Office Equipment | 3,500.00 | |
| 0050 | Motor Vehicles | 6,250.00 | |
| 1003 | Plumbing Material Stocks | 1,750.00 | |
| 1100 | Debtors Control | 1,394.26 | |
| 1200 | Bank Current Account | 204.06 | |
| 1210 | Bank Deposit Account | 1,000.00 | |
| 2100 | Creditors Control | | 1,694.94 |
| 2200 | Sales Tax Control | | 759.33 |
| 2201 | Purchase Tax Control | 252.44 | |
| 2300 | Loans | | 2,000.00 |
| 3000 | Share Capital | | 15,000.00 |
| 4004 | Plumbing Work | | 4,338.99 |
| 5003 | Plumbing Material Purchases | 1,875.00 | |
| 5008 | Small tools & equipment | 1,000.00 | |
| 7103 | General Rates | 1,000.00 | |
| 7200 | Heat, Light and Power | 550.00 | |
| 7504 | Office Stationery | 17.50 | |
| | Totals: | 23,793.26 | 23,793.26 |

The account balances give an overview of the income/expenditure patterns of the business

The totals must match!

# Profit and Loss account

One of the main uses of the information in your accounts is to assess the profitability of your business – and to find ways to make it more profitable. The Profit and Loss account is a key tool for this. It shows the totals of those accounts that are related to trading, and from these calculates:

♦ **Stock**: purchases plus the difference between the opening and closing stocks.

♦ **Gross Profit**: the difference between your sales and goods or raw materials plus the labour and expenses directly incurred in making and selling the goods.

♦ **Net Profit**: Gross Profit minus office costs and other general overheads.

Take note

**You must enter Opening and Closing Stock values at the start and end of periods to get an accurate Stock value in the Profit and Loss account.**

---

G.A. Jones T/A PlumbCrazy
Profit & Loss

|  | Period | | Year to Date | |
|---|---|---|---|---|
| Sales |  |  |  |  |
| Product Sales | 12,021.22 |  | 15,513.75 |  |
| Other Direct Income | 2,904.14 |  | 3,288.84 |  |
|  |  | 14,925.36 |  | 18,802.59 |
| Purchases |  |  |  |  |
| Consumables Purchases | 3,289.10 |  | 3,439.10 |  |
| Stock | 1,800.00 |  | 1,800.00 |  |
|  |  | 5,089.10 |  | 5,239.10 |
| Direct Expenses | 0.00 |  | 0.00 |  |
| Gross Profit/(Loss): |  | 9,836.26 |  | 13,563.49 |
| Overheads |  |  |  |  |
| Gross Wages | 4,000.00 |  | 6,000.00 |  |
| Rent and Rates | 1,080.00 |  | 2,655.00 |  |
| Heat, Light and Power | 203.00 |  | 571.00 |  |
| Motor Expenses | 503.61 |  | 853.61 |  |
| Depreciation | 1,000.00 |  | 1,000.00 |  |
| General Expenses | 532.60 |  | 532.60 |  |
|  |  | 7,319.21 |  | 11,612.21 |
| Net Profit/(Loss): |  | 2,517.15 |  | 1,951.38 |

# End of Period adjustments

Even if you are scrupulous in entering all sales and costs as they occur, your end of period accounts may not give a true picture of the business. Some accounts must be adjusted to reflect the reality of the situation. Stock valuation and depreciation (see page 65) must obviously be handled, and when does a debt become a bad debt?

Another problem is that the expenses entered into the accounts may not relate to the period in question. A business may well pay in arrears for some things and in advance for others. In accounting these are called **accruals** and **prepayments**.

Accruals are monies owing for expenses. Rent, rates, power and phone bills are typically paid in arrears. Even if they are paid on receipt, they are unlikely to coincide exactly with the business's year end. The double-entry solution is to set up an 'accruals' account, and to credit end-of-year bills to this, debiting the matching expense. The true total amount of the expense can then be carried into the Profit and Loss account.

A similar 'prepayments' account can be used in the same way, with debits and credits reversed, to handle pre-paid bills.

## Tip

The Sage system has an Accruals account, (Nominal Code 2109) and a Prepayments (N/C 1103). At the end of the year, outstanding and pre-paid bills should be posted to these through Journal entries (see page 164).

Here the final quarter phone bill of £420 was not paid within the financial year, but the cost is taken into the Profit and Loss calculations by the use of the Accruals account.

| Telephone Account | | | |
|---|---|---|---|
| Debit | £ | Credit | £ |
| Bank | 400 | Profit & Loss | 1720 |
| Bank | 450 | | |
| Bank | 450 | | |
| Accruals (31/12) | 420 | | |
| | 1720 | | |

| Accruals Account | | | |
|---|---|---|---|
| Debit | £ | Credit | £ |
| | | Telephone (31/12) | 420 |

# The Balance Sheet

The Balance Sheet provides a summary of the assets and liabilities of a business — and the two totals must balance, or there is something wrong with the calculations!

Fixed Assets are items which have been bought to be retained within the business (for at least a year), and not for resale at a profit. They are normally items needed to run the business. Any depreciation – or appreciation – is entered into the accounts at the end of the period so that a realistic value is present in the Balance Sheet.

Current Assets are those which will be realised (turned into cash) during the course of the year's trading. They are listed in the Balance Sheet in order of liquidity, with the least liquid at the top. There are two crucial measures that can be drawn from these.

The **Liquidity Ratio** is a measure of how well a business can find cash to meet its short-term debts. It is calculated by:

$$\frac{\text{Current Assets}}{\text{Current Liabilities}}$$

If this is not greater than 1.0, the business is in trouble. In the Sage Balance Sheet display, the **Current Assets less Liabilities** figure gives a similar guide – this must be a positive value or the business could be in trouble.

The **Quick Assets Ratio** is in practice a better guide to the ability of a business to survive a crisis. This uses only the most liquid assets and short-term liabilities:

$$\frac{\text{Cash} + \text{Debtors} + \text{Cashable Deposits}}{\text{Short-Term Current Liabilities}}$$

The question is, 'if you have to raise money in a hurry, what can you turn into cash?'

Take note

These ratios are not calculated by the Sage system, but you can output the figures as a text file and import them into a spreadsheet and perform the calculations there.

## G.A. Jones T/A PlumbCrazy
## Balance Sheet

From: Month 9, September 2002
To: Month 10, October 2002

| | Period | | Year to Date | |
|---|---|---|---|---|
| Fixed Assets | | | | |
| Property | 5,000.00 | | 2,000.00 | |
| Plant and Machinery | 0.00 | | 5,000.00 | |
| Office Equipment | (1,000.00) | | 1,000.00 | |
| Furniture and Fixtures | (500.00) | | 1,000.00 | |
| Motor Vehicles | 0.00 | | 6,250.00 | |
| | | 3,500.00 | | 15,250.00 |
| | | | | |
| Current Assets | | | | |
| Stock | (120.00) | | 1,630.00 | |
| Debtors | (4,197.84) | | 587.77 | |
| Deposits and Cash | 2,961.78 | | 11,511.78 | |
| Bank Account | 8,871.22 | | 4,523.17 | |
| | | 7,515.16 | | 18,252.72 |
| | | | | |
| Current Liabilities | | | | |
| Creditors : Short Term | (596.90) | | (1,396.17) | |
| Creditors : Long Term | 0.00 | | 2,000.00 | |
| VAT Liability | 1,194.95 | | 2,947.51 | |
| | | 598.05 | | 3,551.34 |
| | | | | |
| Current Assets less Liabilities: | | 6,917.11 | | 14,701.38 |
| Net Assets: | | 10,417.11 | | 29,951.38 |
| | | | | |
| Capital & Reserves ②  | | | | ① |
| Share Capital | 5,000.00 | | 25,000.00 | |
| P&L Account | 3,417.11 | | 4,951.38 | |
| | | 8,417.11 | | 29,951.38 |

1    This is the 'bottom line' — the net current worth of the business.

2    This section is sometimes headed 'Financed By' in balance sheets, as it shows where the money has come from to buy the assets.

# Summary

- ❏ Businesses of all sizes and types share a common basis and this is reflected in the structure of the accounts.

- ❏ The purpose of accounts is to track the flow of money through the business, to help its managers run it more efficiently, and to provide legally required information to the Inland Revenue, Customs & Excise and Companies House.

- ❏ Double-entry bookkeeping is based on the concept that every transaction is recorded twice — showing where the money went and where it came from.

- ❏ Where sales and purchases are made on credit, transactions with customers are recorded in the Sales Ledger, those with suppliers in the Purchase Ledger.

- ❏ The Nominal Ledger is the heart of the bookkeeping system. It should contain separate accounts to record each type of income and expenditure.

- ❏ In a manual system the Trial Balance acts as an important check on the accuracy of entries. In Sage systems, it is a useful source of summary information.

- ❏ The Profit and Loss account shows the performance of the business.

- ❏ The Balance Sheet provides a summary of the total assets and liabilities of the business, and shows its current value.

# 2 Sage essentials

# Active Setup

The first essential, of course, is to install Sage Accounts onto your computer and to set it up for your business. This is a simple, straightforward job.

The software will install itself from the CD – just respond the prompts, and let it get on with the job. Unless you choose otherwise, the software will be stored in a folder called *Sage*, within the Program Files folder, and a submenu called *Sage Accounts* will be created in the *Programs* area of the Start menu.

The first time that you run Sage Accounts, the ActiveSetup Wizard will appear. You must work through this to activate the software and to write your key company details into it. Before you start, make sure that you have these things at hand:

◆ The serial number and activation key – you should find these inside the cover of the User's Guide.

◆ Your company's contact details, financial year start date, and VAT registration number.

If you are setting up Sage Accounts for the first time, the wizard will create a basic set of nominal ledger accounts. But different types of business need different structures of accounts – a lawyer won't have retail sales or need to record products in stock – so make sure that you pick the type of company which best matches yours when you reach the My Company stage. The set of accounts probably won't be exactly as you want it, but it will be form a solid basis which you can later add to or adapt to meet your needs (see Chapter 3).

## Basic steps

1   At the Welcome screen click [ Next > ].

2   At Program Activation, enter your serial number and activation key.

3   At My Company, select a set up for a new company, an upgrade or a networked installation.

4   If this is a new set up, pick the type of business.

5   At My Details, enter your contact details.

6   At My Financial Year, pick the month when your year starts.

7   At My VAT Details, enter your VAT number.

8   At Next Steps, click View Setup Checklist.

9   The Help system will run and display the checklist. Read it, and print a copy if required.

10  Back at the wizard, click [ Finish ].

## ActiveSetup Wizard

**ActiveSetup**

### Program Activation

To activate your program you must enter a Serial Number and Activation Key. If you do not have a Serial Number and Activation Key, contact Customer Services, as you must register the program for first time use.

Please enter these details below:

Serial Number: U888863

Activation Key: xxxxxxx

Navigator
- Welcome
- Program Activation
- My Company
- My Details
- My Financial Year
- My VAT Details
- Next Steps

Cancel   < Back   Next >   Finish

**2** Enter the number and key

Click Next after you have completed each stage

---

**3** New, upgrade or networked?

## ActiveSetup Wizard

**ActiveSetup**

### My Company

This section will help you to set up a new company for the first time, convert data from an earlier version, connect to an existing company on a different computer or create an additional company (if you have purchased a multi-company licence).

Navigator
- Welcome
- Program Activation
- My Company
- My Details
- My Financial Year
- My VAT Details
- Next Steps

( ) I would like to create a new company
( ) I am upgrading from an earlier version
( ) I want to use a company located on a networked computer

If you are creating a new company, you can choose a chart of accounts which best fits your needs. From the list below, select the one most appropriate for your business.

General Business - Standard Accounts.

General Business - Standard Accounts.
Accountancy & Financial Practitioners.
Charities or Other Non-Profit Making Organisations.
Medical Practitioners.
Legal Practitioners.
Agricultural Producers or Traders.
Garage and Vehicle Services.
Hotels, Restaurants & Guest Houses.
Building Trade
Transport, Travel & Haulage Services.
I wish to create my own layout of accounts.

Cancel   Finish

**4** What type of company?

---

## Tip

If you realise you have made a mistake at any point, you can click < Back to return to the previous stage.

**ActiveSetup Wizard**

ActiveSetup

Navigator

Welcome
Program Activation
My Company
My Details
My Financial Year
My VAT Details
Next Steps

**My Details**

Next, you need to enter some details about your company as indicated below. The information that you enter here will be used as your business contact details.

| Company Name | G.A. Jones T/A PlumbCrazy |
| Address Line 1 | 12 Coldmain Road |
| Address Line 2 | |
| Town | Plumpton |
| County | |
| Post Code | PL12 2QW |
| Telephone Number | 020 555 1234 |
| Fax Number | |
| E-mail Address | plumbcr |
| Website Address | |

Cancel

**5** Enter your details

**6** Set the start of your year

**ActiveSetup Wizard**

ActiveSetup

Navigator

Welcome
Program Activation
My Company
My Details

**My Financial Year**

You now need to specify the month and year in which your financial year starts.

| Month | May |
| Year | 2002 |

May 2002 - April 2003

...t if you are unsure about your company's financial year

**ActiveSetup Wizard**

ActiveSetup

Navigator

Welcome
Program Activation
My Company
My Details
My Financial Year
My VAT Details
Next Steps

**My VAT Details**

You are now required to supply VAT details about your company.

If your company is VAT registered, enter your VAT registration number below.

VAT Registration Number    123 4567 89

**VAT Cash Accounting Scheme**

The VAT Cash Accounting scheme allows you to account for VAT (output tax) on y... of payments you receive, rather than on tax invoices you issue.

This is different from the normal rules which require you to account for VAT on your sales as they take place or as soon as you issue a VAT invoice, even if you have not been paid by your customer.

☐ Indicate here if your company uses the VAT Cash Accounting scheme

Contact your accountant or your local tax office if you are unsure about which VAT scheme applies.

Cancel          < Back     Next >          Finish

< Back     Next >          Finish

**7** Enter your VAT number

Tick if you use the VAT Cash Accounting scheme

**20**

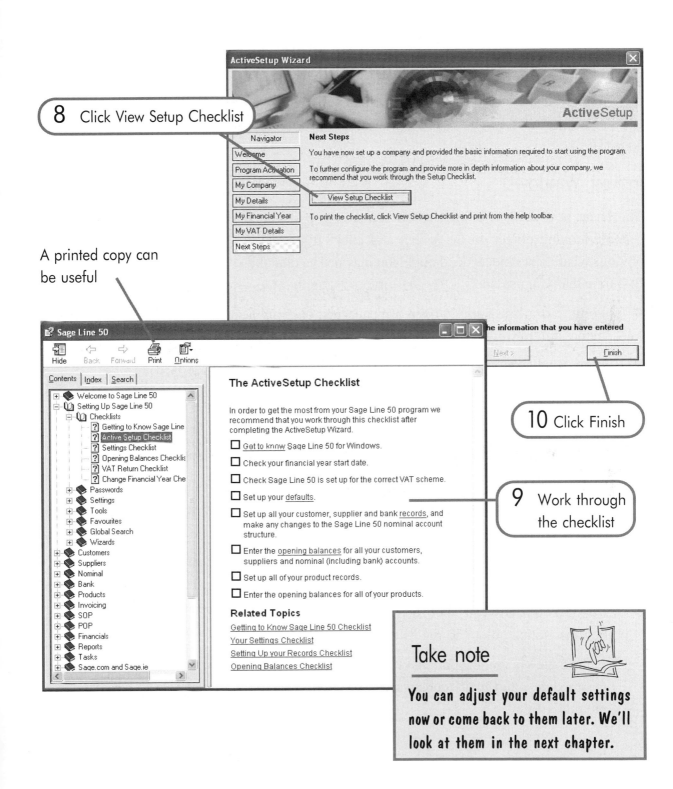

**8** Click View Setup Checklist

A printed copy can be useful

**ActiveSetup Wizard**

ActiveSetup

**Next Steps**

You have now set up a company and provided the basic information required to start using the program.

To further configure the program and provide more in depth information about your company, we recommend that you work through the Setup Checklist.

| Navigator |
| Welcome |
| Program Activation |
| My Company |
| My Details |
| My Financial Year |
| My VAT Details |
| Next Steps |

View Setup Checklist

To print the checklist, click View Setup Checklist and print from the help toolbar.

**Sage Line 50**

Hide    Back    Forward    Print    Options

Contents | Index | Search

- Welcome to Sage Line 50
- Setting Up Sage Line 50
  - Checklists
    - Getting to Know Sage Line
    - Active Setup Checklist
    - Settings Checklist
    - Opening Balances Checklis
    - VAT Return Checklist
    - Change Financial Year Che
  - Passwords
  - Settings
  - Tools
  - Favourites
  - Global Search
  - Wizards
- Customers
- Suppliers
- Nominal
- Bank
- Products
- Invoicing
- SOP
- POP
- Financials
- Reports
- Tasks
- Sage.com and Sage.ie

**The ActiveSetup Checklist**

In order to get the most from your Sage Line 50 program we recommend that you work through this checklist after completing the ActiveSetup Wizard.

☐ Get to know Sage Line 50 for Windows.

☐ Check your financial year start date.

☐ Check Sage Line 50 is set up for the correct VAT scheme.

☐ Set up your defaults.

☐ Set up all your customer, supplier and bank records, and make any changes to the Sage Line 50 nominal account structure.

☐ Enter the opening balances for all your customers, suppliers and nominal (including bank) accounts.

☐ Set up all of your product records.

☐ Enter the opening balances for all of your products.

**Related Topics**

Getting to Know Sage Line 50 Checklist
Your Settings Checklist
Setting Up your Records Checklist
Opening Balances Checklist

the information that you have entered

Next >    Finish

**10** Click Finish

**9** Work through the checklist

**Take note**

You can adjust your default settings now or come back to them later. We'll look at them in the next chapter.

# The screen display

If you are familiar with Windows, much of the screen display and the way you interact with it will be immediately obvious – though the system does have a few little wrinkles all of its own. If you have not met Windows before, here's all you need to know (for now) in a nutshell.

## Instant Windows!

The basic rule is, if you want to do something, point at a suitable-looking object on the screen and click! It's usually obvious what most objects do, though you may need a clue the first time that you use one.

◆ Point to a menu name to open a menu, then click on a menu item to run its command.

◆ If an item has ▶ on the right, a sub-menu will open from it.

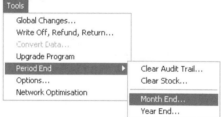

◆ If an item name has ... after it, a module window or dialog box (where you set options) will open when you click on the item.

◆ Many commands can also be reached through toolbar buttons – click on one to run its operation.

In the Sage system, the buttons on the main toolbar open the modules, and their toolbars perform tasks with the module's data.

Tip

Play with the system before you start to use it for real. Start the Sage system, click on the File menu and click Open Demo data. Explore and experiment with these files to get the hang of the system.

After you have entered data or choices in a dialog box, click OK to save your settings and close the box.

Point to a name to open a menu

Click on a command to run it

Click to open a module window

Title bar

Click to perform tasks

Window control

Maximise

Close

Menu bar

Minimise

Toolbars

Sage Line 50 Accountant - Stationery & Computer Mart UK

File  Edit  View  Modules  Settings  Tools  Favourites  Window  Help

New
Open
Close          Ctrl+F4
Backup...

Import...
Maintenance...

Restore...

Send

Log Off

Exit

al  Bank  Products  Invoicing  Financials  Period End  Reports  Tasks  sage.com  Help

Nominal Ledger

D C

Activity  Aged  Invoice  Credit  Charges  Phone  Labels

(All Records)

Credit

Customers

(All Records)

A/C                N
A1D001          A
ABS001          A
BBS001          B
BRI001           F
BRO001          B
BUS001          B
CASH001        C
CGS001          C
COM001          C
DST001           J
FGL001           F
GRA001          G
HAU001          H

Search        Swap

Customer - Bronson Inc

Details  Defaults  Credit Control  Sales  Graphs  Activity  Memo

A/C         BRO001                                    Balance              0.00

Name       Bronson Inc                                Amount Paid      16775.25

Credit Limit       4000.00                            Turnover YTD     14742.39

| No | Tp | Date | Refn | Details | Amount | O/S | Debit | Credit |
|----|----|------|------|---------|--------|-----|-------|--------|
|    | 4 SI | 31/12/2000 | O/BAL | Opening Balance | 230.00 | | 230.00 | |
|    | 222 SI | 29/01/2001 | 13 | JP020 Jet Printer | 1026.00 | | 1026.00 | |
|    | 223 SI | 29/01/2001 | 13 | PC Combo Pack 2 | 3087.50 | | 3087.50 | |
|    | 224 SI | 29/01/2001 | 13 | JP020 Jet Printer Cartr | 28.50 | | 28.50 | |
|    | 225 SI | 29/01/2001 | 13 | JP010 Jet Printer Cartr | 34.20 | | 34.20 | |

| Future | Current | 1 Month(s) | 2 Month(s) | 3 Month(s) | Older |
|--------|---------|-----------|-----------|-----------|-------|
| 0.00 | 0.00 | 0.00 | 0.00 | 0.00 | 0.00 |

Tidy List     Range

Save     Discard     Delete     Back     Next     Print List                    Close

Bank A...

Sage Line 50 Accountant                                              09/07/2002   January 2001   1 63

Status bar

Click on a tab to open its panel

Click on an item to select it

Click to close a module window

Restore minimised window

# Window layout

Every application runs in a window, and documents or modules are displayed in windows within the application. Both types of windows are controlled in the same way.

Use the buttons in the top right to control the window size.

🔲 **Minimise** the window to its title bar only.

🔲 **Maximise** an application window to fill the screen, or a module window to fill the working area. When a module is maximised, its title bar and toolbar are merged with those of the main window.

🔲 Set the window to **Restore** mode. It can then be moved by *dragging* its title bar, or resized by dragging an edge or corner.

To drag a screen object, point to it, hold the left mouse button down and move the mouse. The object will follow the cursor.

🔲 **Closes** the window.

## Working with multiple windows

Any number of application or module windows can be open at the same time. This allows you to work very flexibly, but can result in confused and cluttered screen displays. If you can't see what you are doing, close unwanted windows (you can always reopen them again) or use the commands on the Windows menu to tidy the screen, or to bring a window to the front.

**Basic steps**

1  Open some windows!

❑  Tidying the layout

2  Point to the Window menu.

3  Click Cascade or Tile.

❑  Moving to a window

4  If you can see part of a window, click on it.

*Or*

5  Point to the Window menu.

6  Open windows are listed at the bottom – click the one you want.

Take note

Module windows are normally opened and used in Restore mode. If you maximise one module window, all module windows are maximised until you switch back to Restore mode.

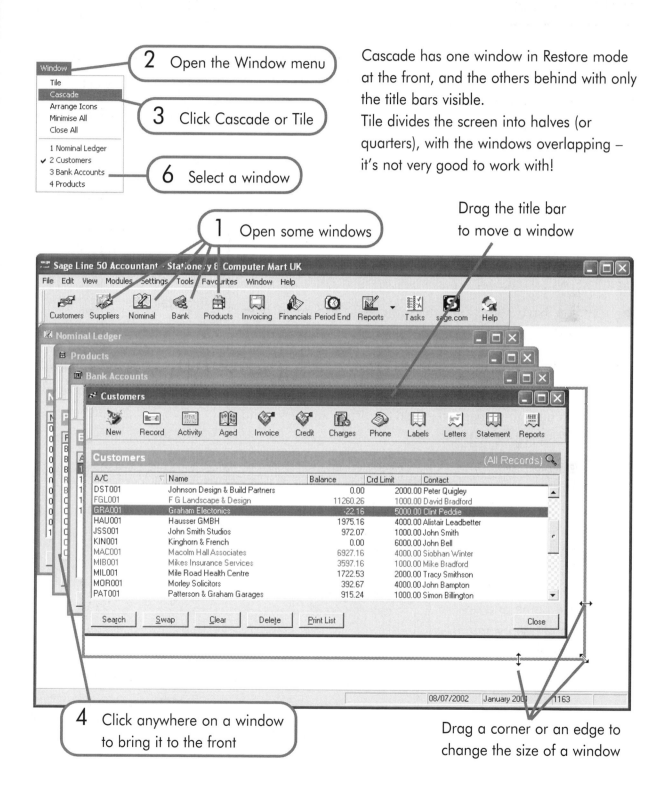

**2** Open the Window menu

**Window**
- Tile
- Cascade
- Arrange Icons
- Minimise All
- Close All
- 1 Nominal Ledger
- ✓ 2 Customers
- 3 Bank Accounts
- 4 Products

**3** Click Cascade or Tile

**6** Select a window

Cascade has one window in Restore mode at the front, and the others behind with only the title bars visible.

Tile divides the screen into halves (or quarters), with the windows overlapping – it's not very good to work with!

**1** Open some windows

Drag the title bar to move a window

Sage Line 50 Accountant - Stationery & Computer Mart UK

File  Edit  View  Modules  Settings  Tools  Favourites  Window  Help

Customers  Suppliers  Nominal  Bank  Products  Invoicing  Financials  Period End  Reports  Tasks  sage.com  Help

Nominal Ledger

Products

Bank Accounts

**Customers**

New  Record  Activity  Aged  Invoice  Credit  Charges  Phone  Labels  Letters  Statement  Reports

**Customers** (All Records)

| A/C | Name | Balance | Crd Limit | Contact |
|-----|------|---------|-----------|---------|
| DST001 | Johnson Design & Build Partners | 0.00 | 2000.00 | Peter Quigley |
| FGL001 | F G Landscape & Design | 11260.26 | 1000.00 | David Bradford |
| GRA001 | Graham Electonics | -22.16 | 5000.00 | Clint Peddie |
| HAU001 | Hausser GMBH | 1975.16 | 4000.00 | Alistair Leadbetter |
| JSS001 | John Smith Studios | 972.07 | 1000.00 | John Smith |
| KIN001 | Kinghorn & French | 0.00 | 6000.00 | John Bell |
| MAC001 | Macolm Hall Associates | 6927.16 | 4000.00 | Siobhan Winter |
| MIB001 | Mikes Insurance Services | 3597.16 | 1000.00 | Mike Bradford |
| MIL001 | Mile Road Health Centre | 1722.53 | 2000.00 | Tracy Smithson |
| MOR001 | Morley Solicitors | 392.67 | 4000.00 | John Bampton |
| PAT001 | Patterson & Graham Garages | 915.24 | 1000.00 | Simon Billington |

Search  Swap  Clear  Delete  Print List  Close

08/07/2002  January 2001  1163

**4** Click anywhere on a window to bring it to the front

Drag a corner or an edge to change the size of a window

# Entering data

For the most part, data is entered and edited using the standard Windows techniques – i.e. type in the text, using backspace to rub out errors, and the arrow keys to move around within it to erase or add characters. There are also a few special techniques.

## Text items

You will very rarely write continuous text when doing the accounts. Almost all text will be short items – names, addresses and other details of new customers, entries on invoices, and the like. Each of these items will normally go into a separate field (text box) on screen.

- ◆ If you have something that you want to spread over several lines, such as the details in a service invoice, press [Enter] at the end of each line.

- ◆ When you want to go to the next field, press [⇤⇥].

- ◆ If you need to go back to a field to correct an entry, hold [⇧] and press [⇤⇥].

Tip

To correct an error, move the cursor to it, press [←] to delete backwards or [Delete] to delete forwards, then type the correction. Don't try to overtype — new characters are always inserted.

Each item of data goes into a field – usually a single word or value, but sometimes taking several lines

Most things only need typing once. Here, selecting REVGREEN from the A/C Ref pulled in the name and address that had been stored in the Customer record.

*Service Invoice window:*

Details | Order Details | Footer Details | Payment Details

Rev Green
The Old Vicarage
Church Road
Plumpton

Type: Invoice
Format: Service
Date: 09/07/2002
A/C: REVGREEN

Service Invoice
Inv.No. <AutoNumber>
Order No
Item No. Item 1 of 2

| Details | Amount | Net | V.A.T. |
|---|---|---|---|
| Central heating overhaul | | | |
| Clean and service boiler | | | |
| Adjust leaking radiator valves (x3) | 65.00 | 65.00 | 10.81 |
| | 0.00 | 0.00 | 0.00 |

| TC | Rate | Description | Net | VAT |
|---|---|---|---|---|
| 1 | 17.50 | Standard Rate transacti | 65.00 | 10.81 |

Total: 65.00 / 10.81
Carriage: 0.00 / 0.00
Gross: 75.81

Save | Discard | Print | Close

# Easy data entry

The Sage system provides easy ways to enter numbers, dates and information that is already in your files.

## Numbers

When you go to a number field, you will usually see ▦ by the side. Click on this and a small calculator will appear. Click on the digits to enter a number or use it as a calculator to work out discounts or other values. Click = when you have done.

## Dates

The Program Date (normally the current date, but see page 46) is entered automatically into date fields. If you want to change it, click ▦ to open the 'calendar' display. Select the date and press [Esc] or click elsewhere on screen to close the calendar. These dates appear in Day/Month order; elsewhere in the system you'll sometimes find them in Month/Day order.

## Drop-down lists

When you are creating an invoice and need the details of a customer, then – as long as it is already in the system – the information can be pulled out by selecting from the list that drops down from the ▤ at the side of the field. Accounts, names of suppliers, product details and similar data can likewise be selected from drop-down lists.

Backspace

Clear number

Clear last entry in calculation

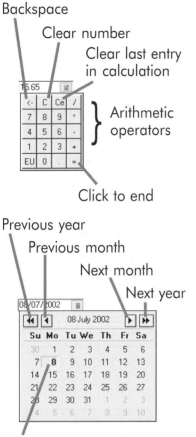

Arithmetic operators

Click to end

Previous year

Previous month

Next month

Next year

Click to select day

Take note

The ▦ ▦ ▤ buttons only appear when the cursor is in the fields.

Click to drop down the list

Scroll the list and select

Click OK

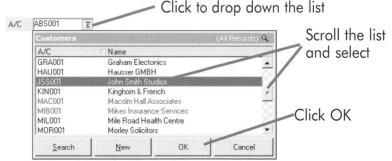

# Selections

Before you can edit, delete or in any other way process a record or account, it must be selected. This is done by clicking anywhere on its line in its window.

## Multiple selection

In the Customers, Suppliers, Nominal, Products and Invoicing windows, any number of records can be selected at any one time – and once selected, a record stays selected until you deselect it. This is a valuable feature as it allows you to process records in batches.

For example, one of your first jobs when setting up the Sage system will be to work through the Nominal accounts entering opening balances. If you first go through the list and select all the relevant ones, you can then work steadily through the opening balances routine without having to keep coming back to select the next record.

Take note

**Multiple selection has its disadvantages! As you scroll down the list, it is very easy to forget that a record is selected higher up. When you select another record and start to process it, you then see the 'wrong' details on the screen. And, do take care when deleting ...**

Click to select or deselect

Filter the displayed list. See page 86.

**Nominal Ledger**

| | | | | | |
|---|---|---|---|---|---|
| New | Record | Activity | Journals | COA | Reports |

**Nominal Ledger**                                (All Records)

| N/C | Name | Debit | Credit |
|---|---|---|---|
| 0031 | Office Equipment Depreciation | | |
| 0040 | Furniture and Fixtures | | |
| 0041 | Furniture/Fixture Depreciation | | |
| 0050 | Motor Vehicles | | |
| 0051 | Motor Vehicles Depreciation | | |
| 0060 | Computer software | | |
| 1001 | Stock | | |
| 1002 | Work in Progress | | |
| 1003 | Finished Goods | | |
| 1100 | Debtors Control Account | | |

| Search | Swap | Clear | Delete | Print List | Close |
|---|---|---|---|---|---|

Inverts the selection, so that those currently selected are deselected, and vice versa.

Deselect all records

Delete the selected record(s)

# Single selection

Only one record can be selected at a time in the Bank and Financial modules. Clicking on a record automatically deselects any other selection. Similarly, only one item can be selected in the panels that display the details of records. In most of these cases, 'selecting' a record or item does no more than highlight it for easier identification, as they cannot be edited or processed.

When several records have been selected before opening a viewing or editing panel, you can move between them by clicking the `Back` and `Next` buttons.

The ⊞ icon shows that you are looking at a summary. Double-click anywhere on the line to display its details.

# Task Manager

The Task Manager can help you to monitor the status of accounts, and to keep track of the jobs that need doing.

The Tasks buttons down the left side are used to move between the sections. The main window is divided into a 'tree' panel, containing the folders for sub-sections, and a 'list' panel where tasks and other items are displayed.

Only the To Do and Bills sections are interactive; the rest simply display information. In the Accounts Due, Accounts Status, Recurring and Invoices you can see the appropriate records, but you cannot do anything with them – to chase the late payment or pay the overdue invoice, you must return to the main accounts window.

1 Click .

❑ The To Do list

2 Click the To Do button.

3 Click [New].

4 Set the Type and Date and enter a Description and Notes if wanted.

5 Click [OK].

6 Open the Current or Overdue Tasks folder and double-click on a task to open its panel.

7 Tick Task Complete when it's done!

**2** Click To Do

**3** Click New

**6** Open a folder and double-click an item

**Sage Task Manager**

File  Tasks  Settings  Help

New  Open  Delete  Pay  Properties

Tasks

To Do List

- Current Tasks
- Overdue Task
- Completed Tas

| Name | Date Due | Project |
|------|----------|---------|
| Mid-month statements | 15/07/2002 | General Reminde |

To Do
Bills
Accounts Due
Account Status
Company

**To Do Entry**

Details

Type        Reconcile bank account
Date Due    31/07/2002
Description End of month reconciliation      ☐ Task Complete
Delegate To MANAGER

Notes

To be done by Joyce (trainee). Henry to check.

OK    Cancel

**4** Enter details

**7** Job Done!

**5** Click OK

## Basic steps

❑ Bills

1 Click the Bills button.

2 Click 📄 New.

3 Select the Nominal account and enter the Details.

4 Click OK.

5 Select the bill and click 🖉 Pay.

6 Select the Bank account and enter the Details.

7 Click OK.

Double-click an item to open its Properties panel

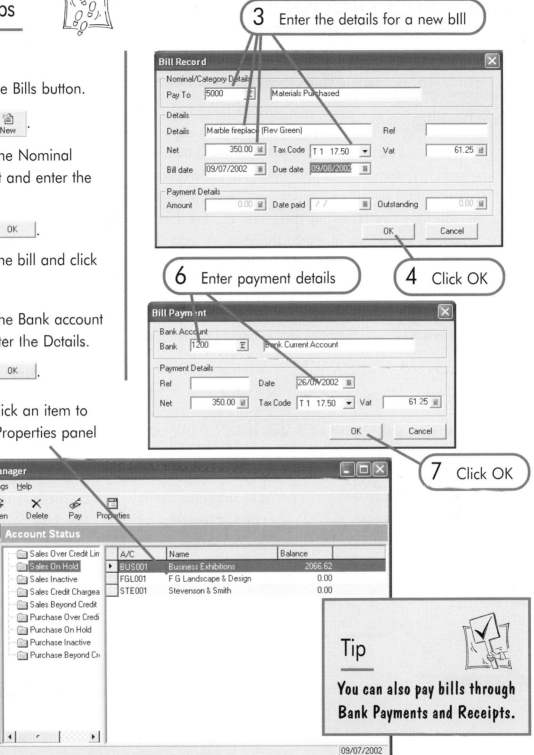

**3** Enter the details for a new bIll

**Bill Record**

Nominal/Category Details

Pay To  5000        Materials Purchased

Details

Details  Marble fireplace (Rev Green)       Ref

Net  350.00   Tax Code  T 1  17.50 ▼   Vat  61.25

Bill date  09/07/2002   Due date  09/08/2002

Payment Details

Amount  0.00   Date paid  / /   Outstanding  0.00

OK      Cancel

**6** Enter payment details

**4** Click OK

**Bill Payment**

Bank Account

Bank  1200        Bank Current Account

Payment Details

Ref        Date  26/07/2002

Net  350.00   Tax Code  T 1  17.50 ▼  Vat  61.25

OK      Cancel

**7** Click OK

**Sage Task Manager**

File  Tasks  Settings  Help

New  Open  Delete  Pay  Properties

Tasks

**Account Status**

- Sales Over Credit Lim
- Sales On Hold
- Sales Inactive
- Sales Credit Chargea
- Sales Beyond Credit
- Purchase Over Credi
- Purchase On Hold
- Purchase Inactive
- Purchase Beyond Cr

| A/C | Name | Balance |
|-----|------|---------|
| BUS001 | Business Exhibitions | 2066.62 |
| FGL001 | F G Landscape & Design | 0.00 |
| STE001 | Stevenson & Smith | 0.00 |

To Do

Bills

Accounts Due

Account Status

Company

09/07/2002

### Tip

**You can also pay bills through Bank Payments and Receipts.**

# Data Maintenance

With good habits – and a little luck – you may never need to use these routines, but you should know about them just in case!

## Error checking

The error checking routine will scan your files, and the links between them, to make sure that your data is in good order. It will then give you a list of errors, warnings and comments. There shouldn't be any errors! If there are, the Fix facility should be able to correct them, but if this doesn't work it is almost certainly means that your files are corrupted and should be restored from the backups (see page 36).

Warnings and comments, if any, will normally relate to minor inconsistencies which you should be able to correct from within the system.

## Compression

When transactions, records and other data items are deleted – either through Corrections or, more commonly, as part of clearing the audit trail (see page 114) – the data initially remains in the files, but flagged so that it is ignored by the system. The compression routine works through the files, removing all 'deleted' data. It is something that should be done from time to time to save disk space.

1 Open the File menu and click Maintenance.

❑ Error checking

2 Click ⌈ Check Data ⌉.

3 If there are Errors, click ⌈ Fix ⌉.

4 Read the messages on the Warnings and Comments tabs, making a note of any that need attention.

5 Click ⌈ Close ⌉.

❑ Compression

6 Click ⌈ Compress Data ⌉.

7 If you only want to compress certain files, clear the Compress All Data Files checkbox and select the files.

8 Click ⌈ Compress ⌉.

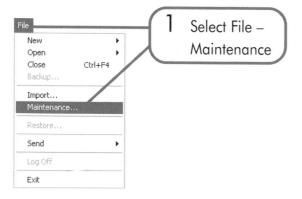

1 Select File – Maintenance

## Tip

**Compressing very large files can take a while. To save time, select only those where you know there is most deleted data to remove.**

32

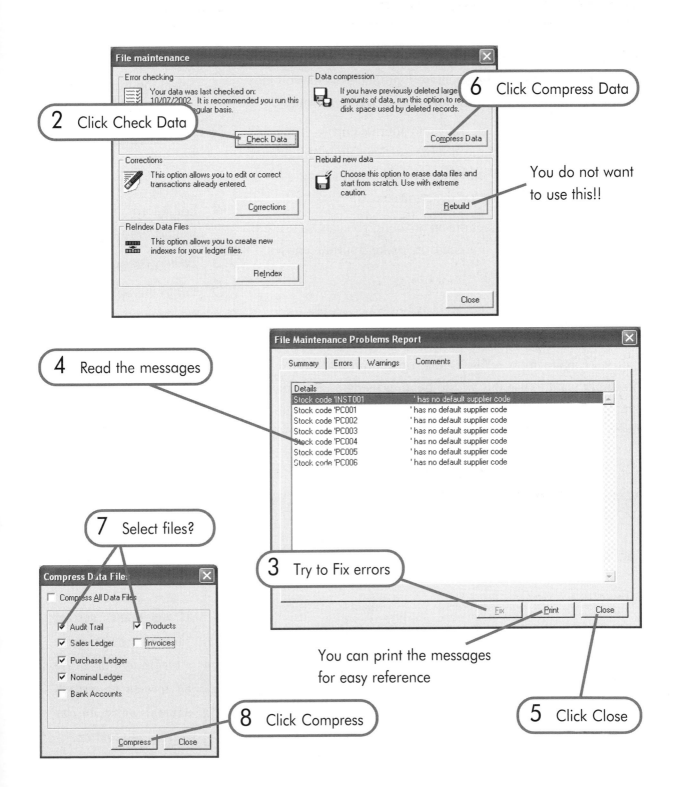

**File maintenance**

Error checking
Your data was last checked on:
10/07/2002. It is recommended you run this ... regular basis.

Check Data

2 Click Check Data

Data compression
If you have previously deleted large ... amounts of data, run this option to re... disk space used by deleted records.

Compress Data

6 Click Compress Data

Corrections
This option allows you to edit or correct transactions already entered.

Corrections

Rebuild new data
Choose this option to erase data files and start from scratch. Use with extreme caution.

Rebuild

You do not want to use this!!

ReIndex Data Files
This option allows you to create new indexes for your ledger files.

ReIndex

Close

4 Read the messages

**File Maintenance Problems Report**

Summary | Errors | Warnings | Comments

Details
Stock code 'INST001        ' has no default supplier code
Stock code 'PC001         ' has no default supplier code
Stock code 'PC002         ' has no default supplier code
Stock code 'PC003         ' has no default supplier code
Stock code 'PC004         ' has no default supplier code
Stock code 'PC005         ' has no default supplier code
Stock code 'PC006         ' has no default supplier code

Fix    Print    Close

3 Try to Fix errors

You can print the messages for easy reference

5 Click Close

7 Select files?

**Compress Data Files**

☐ Compress All Data Files

☑ Audit Trail      ☑ Products
☑ Sales Ledger    ☐ Invoices
☑ Purchase Ledger
☑ Nominal Ledger
☐ Bank Accounts

Compress    Close

8 Click Compress

# Corrections

If an error is made when entering a transaction, or a transaction is cancelled after it has been entered into the system, you may be able to delete or edit it through the Corrections routine.

♦ Bank transfers (page 107) and Journal entries (page 64), which have matching double-entries, cannot be deleted and you can only edit non-critical information, such as Department codes and descriptive text.

♦ If you cannot correct the errors here, you can issue credit notes to nullify invoices or make Journal entries to reverse mispostings.

## Rebuild

Not to be used lightly, this erases all your data files so that you can start again from scratch! The only time that you would probably want to use this would be after using dummy data to get the hang of the system. Rebuild will clear away the rubbish ready to start work in earnest.

## Basic steps

1 Click [ Corrections ].

2 Select the transaction and click [ Edit ].

3 Click [ Delete ] to remove the entry.

*Or*

4 Edit information in the Details area as needed.

❑ Editing Amounts

5 Go to the Split tab, select an item and click [ Edit ].

6 Edit the Details and Amounts as needed.

7 Click [ Close ] to leave the split record panel.

8 Click [ Save ].

9 Click [ Close ].

**Posting Error Corrections**

| No | Tp | Date | Account | Bank/N/C | Ref | Details | Net | Tax |
|---|---|---|---|---|---|---|---|---|
| 1127 | PP | 27/04/2001 | WIS002 | 1200 | | Purchase Paym | 4292.05 | 0.00 |
| 1128 | PI | 27/04/2001 | CON001 | | 33 | Rubber Bands · | 834.30 | 142.38 |
| 1139 | PI | 27/04/2001 | M^N001 | | 34 | MTH1000 Moth | 6768.00 | 1154.80 |
| 1151 | PI | 27/04/2001 | UN I001 | | 35 | Letter Trays - 3 | 128.48 | 21.92 |
| 1153 | PI | 27/04/2001 | WI 002 | | 36 | Whiteboard - D | 1633.86 | 278.79 |
| 1162 | SC | 06/06/2001 | GR 001 | | | | 4000.00 | 700.00 |
| 1163 | SI | 07/06/2001 | GR 001 | | | | 450.00 | 78.75 |
| 1164 | SR | 09/07/2002 | AB 001 | 1200 | | Sales Receipt | 2533.31 | 0.00 |
| 1165 | SA | 09/07/2002 | BB 001 | 1200 | | Payment on Ac | 4309.77 | 0.00 |
| 1166 | SR | 09/07/2002 | MIB 01 | 1200 | | Sales Receipt | 3597.16 | 0.00 |
| 1167 | SR | 09/07/2002 | VID 1 | 1200 | | Sales Receipt | 2041.66 | 0.00 |
| 1168 | SR | 09/07/2002 | FGL 1 | 1200 | | Sales Receipt | 11260.26 | 0.00 |
| 1169 | SR | 09/07/2002 | STE 1 | 1200 | | Sales Receipt | 1562.75 | 0.00 |
| 1170 | SR | 09/07/2002 | SWA 1 | 1200 | | Sales Receipt | 1598.83 | 0.00 |

[ Find ]  [ Edit ]                                          [ Close ]

2 Select an item and click Edit

## Tip

**If you cannot correct the error, you can issue a credit note to nullify an invoice or make a Journal entry to reverse a misposting.**

Displays summary only

**4** Edit Details?

**Take note**

**If it is written in grey, you can't change it!**

---

**Number 1139  Purchase Invoice**  ⊠

Details | Amounts | Splits

Details

Account  MCN001  ⬚

Date due  27/05/2002  ⬚

Details  MTH1000 Motherboard

Reference  34

Posted by  MANAGER

Date  27/04/2001  ⬚

Bank Rec. Date  / /  ⬚

Posting  14/09/2001  ⬚

_Save_    _Edit_    _Delete_

**3**  Click Delete

**8**  Click Save

---

**Number 1139, Purchase Invoice**  ⊠

Details | Amounts | Splits

| No | N/C | Details | Net | T/c | Tax |
|----|-----|---------|-----|-----|-----|
| 1139 | 5001 | MTH1000 Motherboard | 270.00 | T1 | 46.07 |
| 1140 | 5001 | MTH2000 Motherboard | 360.00 | T1 | 61.42 |
| 1141 | 5001 | DIMM 64mb 100Mhz | 387.00 | T1 | 66.04 |
| 1142 | 5001 | 10gb Hard Drive | 288.00 | T1 | 49.14 |
| 1143 | 5001 | 30gb Hard Drive | 648.00 | T1 | 110.57 |
| 1144 | 5001 | MTH3000 Motherboard | 450.00 | T1 | 76.78 |
| 1145 | 5001 | DIMM 128m 100Mhz | 738.00 | T1 | 125.92 |
| 1146 | 5001 | DIMM 32m 100Mhz | 198.00 | T1 | 33.78 |
| 1147 | 5001 | SIMM 64mb 100Mhz | 549.00 | T1 | 93.68 |

_Save_    _Edit_    _Delete_    Close

**5**  Select and click Edit

**9**  Click Close

---

**Number 1145, Purchase Invoice**  ⊠

Details

N/C  5001  ⬚

Details  DIMM 128mb 100Mhz

Date  27/04/2001

Department  2 Purchasing  ▼

Ex.Ref

**6**  Edit details or amounts

Amounts

Net  638  ⬚  Tax  125.92  ⬚  T/C  T1 17.50  ▼  Paid  0.00  ⬚

| <- | C | Ce | / |
|----|---|----|----|
| 7 | 8 | 9 | x |
| 4 | 5 | 6 | - |
| 1 | 2 | 3 | + |
| EU | 0 | . | = |

Flag

☐  VAT Reconciled

Alloc

| Tp | Date | Ref | Details | Amount |
|----|------|-----|---------|--------|

_Edit_    Close

**7**  Click Close

35

# Backups

You must get into the habit of backing up your files regularly. The Sage system is very reliable but computers get stolen or damaged, and hard disks can fail. Would your business survive if it lost all its accounts data? More specifically, how much data can you afford to lose and still survive?

A backup file will store that precious accounts data – it will also hold your configuration settings and company details.

♦ Backups should be made daily, or weekly, depending on the number of transactions going through the accounts.

♦ They should be on removable media, stored away from the computer, ideally in a fireproof safe in another building.

♦ Each backup should be on a separate disk or tape, so that if one is destroyed or corrupted, there is a recent previous version to work from. If you do daily backups, you might have a set of 5 (or 6) that you recycle weekly.

## Restoring files

If the worst happens, you can easily recreate your files – if necessary on a new computer – using the Restore routine.

You will lose all the transactions that have been recorded since the last backup, but if you have been backing up regularly, they should not take long to re-enter.

1 Open the File menu and select Backup...

2 You will be asked if you want to check the files – click Yes if you haven't checked them recently.

3 Select the drive and folder, and edit the name, if you need to identify it more clearly.

4 Select the files to backup.

5 Click ⬚ OK ⬚ and wait while files are saved.

❑ Restore

6 Open the File menu and select Restore...

7 Click Yes at the Confirm prompt.

8 Select the drive/folder and file and click ⬚ OK ⬚.

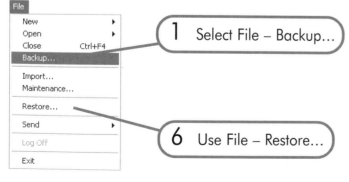

1 Select File – Backup...

6 Use File – Restore...

2 Check files first?

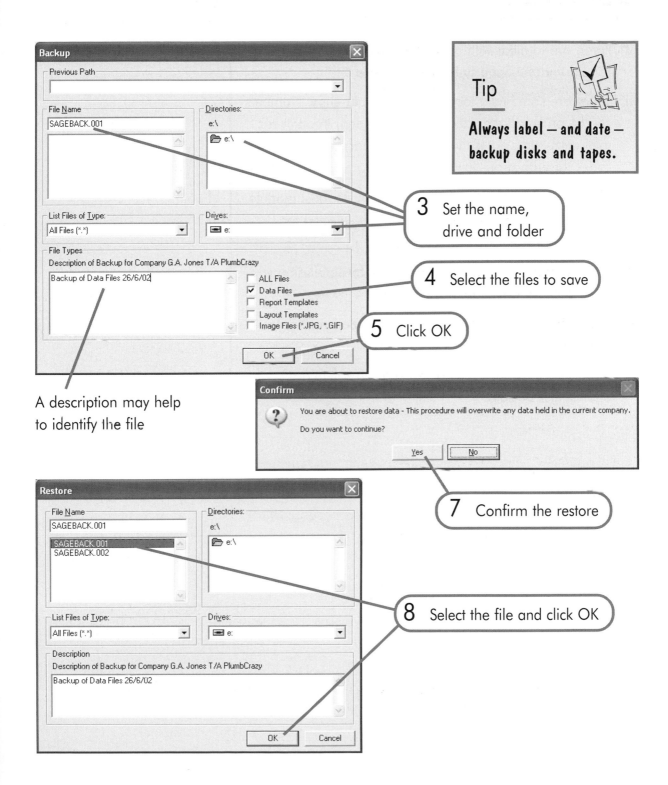

# Summary

❑ If you are familiar with other Windows applications, you should find the Sage systems easy to use.

❑ There are some neat tools to simplify data entry. Numbers can be entered (after calculating, if needed) through a mini-calculator; dates through a calendar; and account codes through drop-down lists.

❑ Records are selected by clicking on them. In most module windows, any number of records can be selected for processing in a batch.

❑ You may find the Task Manager useful for reminding you of or identifying jobs that need doing.

❑ The Data Maintenance routines should keep your data files in good order...

❑ ... but you must take regular Backups, to safeguard against loss of data.

# 3 The Settings

# Company Preferences

You probably set up your basic Company Preferences during installation. Other default settings for customers and suppliers, the organisation of the business into departments and of products into categories, may also have been set up then. Any information that was not entered then, or that has changed since, can be put in through the Settings options.

## Departments

If your company is organised into departments, or has several branches, these can be written into the Sage system and used when creating invoices and analysing activity. Even if there are no actual departments, analysing the business by its areas of work will show the relative profitability of each.

## Basic steps

1 Open the Settings menu and select Company Preferences...

2 On the Address panel, enter your contact details – they will be used on your letters and invoices.

3 The Labels panel is probably best left alone until you really know the system. This controls which fields are included in the customer, supplier and product records.

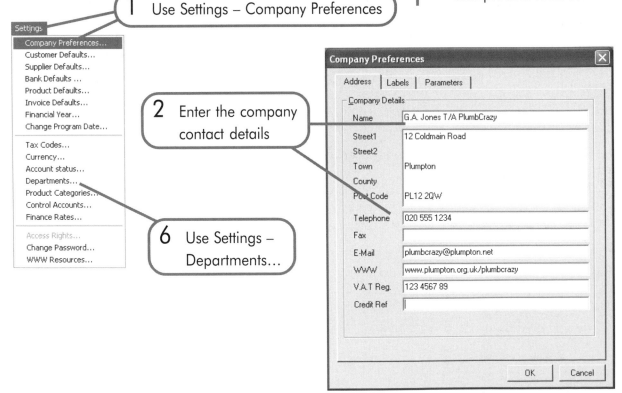

1 Use Settings – Company Preferences

2 Enter the company contact details

6 Use Settings – Departments...

**4** On the Parameters panel, set your VAT defaults and other options as required.

**5** Click 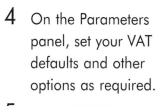 OK .

❑ Departments

**6** From the Settings menu select Departments...

**7** Select an unused department and click Edit .

**8** Enter a name and click OK .

**9** Repeat steps 6 and 7 for all your departments, then click Close .

**3** Leave the Labels alone!

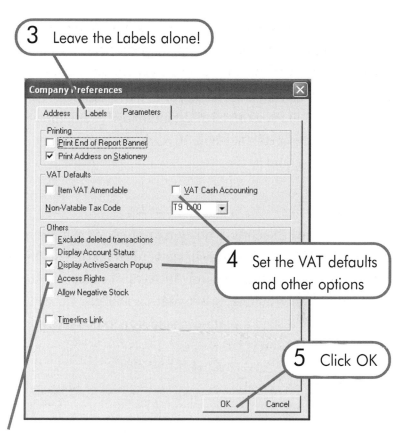

**4** Set the VAT defaults and other options

**5** Click OK

If you have several users, turn on Access Rights, then go to Settings – Access Rights... and give each user a name and password

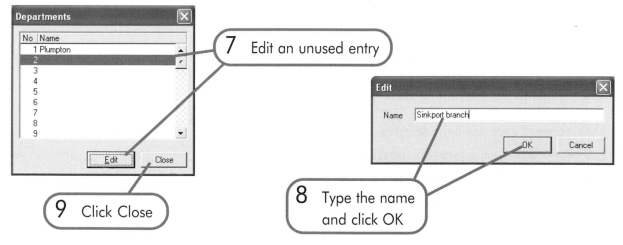

**7** Edit an unused entry

**9** Click Close

**8** Type the name and click OK

# Customers and suppliers

The Customers and Suppliers Defaults follow the same pattern.

## Account Terms

What is your normal credit limit for a new customer? When is payment due? Do you offer a discount for early settlement? The defaults settings are for a simple 30 days' payment with no early settlement discount.

## Ageing

Chasing debts efficiently is a key part of good cashflow management. Aged Analysis groups overdue debts, with the default settings in multiples of 30 days. You can switch to calendar month grouping, or set your own limits. How old is a debt before you send a reminder, and how much older before you send for the lawyers?

## Basic steps

1 Open the Settings menu and select Customer Defaults…

2 On the Record panel, set the due days and type the settlement Terms as they should appear on invoices.

3 For the Ageing, set new limits or switch to Monthly if required.

4 With customers, there is a Statements panel with descriptions, which could be edited if desired.

5 Click ___OK___.

6 Open the Settings menu and select Supplier Defaults…

7 Repeat steps 2, 3 and 5 for your suppliers.

## Take note

The settings here are only *defaults*. They will be in place when you reach the relevant stage in creating a new Customer or Supplier record or invoice, but can then be changed if necessary.

**1** Use Settings – Customer Defaults...

**4** Edit the descriptions?

**2** What are your terms of trade?

**3** How do you want to group overdue accounts?

**5** Click OK

Settings

Company Preferences...
Customer Defaults...
Supplier Defaults...
Bank Defaults ...
Product Defaults...
Invoice Defaults...
Financial Year...
Change Program Date...

Tax Codes...
Currency...
Account status...
Departments...
Product Categories...
Control Accounts...
Finance Rates...

Access Rights...
Change Password...
WWW Resources...

**Customer Defaults**

Record | Statements | Ageing

Terms
Credit Limit          500.00      Payment Due Days   30
Sett. Discount          5.00      Sett. Due Days      7
Terms

Defaults
Currency       1   Pound Sterling
Std Tax Code   T1 17.50        Def. N/C   4000
Department     0

Discounts
Disc. %         0.00

Account status
Default        0 Open

OK    Cancel

**Customer Defaults**

Record | Statements | Ageing

Ageing Type
○ Calendar Monthly Ageing
● Period Ageing

                      From    To
Aged Period 1          30     59    Days
Aged Period 2          60     89    Days
Aged Period 3          90    119    Days
Aged Period 4         120    Days plus

☐ Start Period Ageing on first day of month after Transaction date?

Defaults
☐ Include future totals in balance

OK    Cancel

# Products

Though stock control modules are only present in the Accountant Plus and Financial Controller packages, all Sage systems can handle details of the products that you make, sell or supply as part of your service-based work. This information is used when generating invoices and credit notes – selecting a product's code will pull in its description, price, tax rate and default order quantity.

There are two Settings options:

♦   The default will be used when you create records with the New Product Wizard (see page 124). If you pick the most common settings, few will need to be changed when they are applied to a record.

♦   Products can be organised into categories. This can be useful for analysing your business activities.

(see page 124)

## Basic steps

❑   Default settings

1   Open the Settings menu and select Product Defaults...

2   Select the most common settings for Nominal Code, Tax Code, Unit of Sale, Category and Department.

3   Set the number of decimal places to show for Quantities and Prices on invoices.

4   Click   OK  .

---

**Settings**
Company Preferences...
Customer Defaults...
Supplier Defaults...
Bank Defaults ...
Product Defaults...
Invoice Defaults...
Financial Year...
Change Program Date...

Tax Codes...
Currency...
Account status...
Departments...
Product Categories...
Control Accounts...
Finance Rates...

Access Rights...
Change Password...
WWW Resources...

**1   Use Settings – Product Defaults...**

**Product Defaults**

| Details |

Defaults
Nominal Code    4000
Tax Code        T1  17.50
Unit of Sale
Category        1 Bathroom fittings
Department      1 Plumpton

**2   Pick the most common settings**

Decimal Precison
Quantity D.P.   2
Unit D.P.       2

**3   How many decimal places?**

**4   Click OK**

OK     Cancel

---

□ Categories

**5** Open the Settings menu and select Product Categories...

**6** Select an unused category, click [ Edit ].

**7** Enter a name and click [ OK ].

**8** Repeat steps 6 and 7 for all your new categories, then click [ Close ].

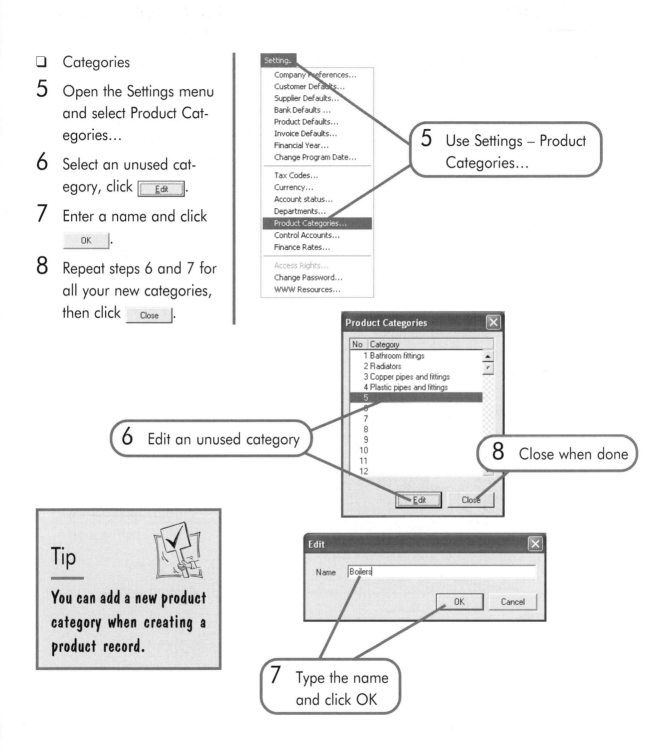

Settings

Company Preferences...
Customer Defaults...
Supplier Defaults...
Bank Defaults ...
Product Defaults...
Invoice Defaults...
Financial Year...
Change Program Date...

Tax Codes...
Currency...
Account status...
Departments...
Product Categories...
Control Accounts...
Finance Rates...

Access Rights...
Change Password...
WWW Resources...

**5** Use Settings – Product Categories...

**Product Categories**

| No | Category |
|----|----------|
| 1 | Bathroom fittings |
| 2 | Radiators |
| 3 | Copper pipes and fittings |
| 4 | Plastic pipes and fittings |
| 5 | |
| 6 | |
| 7 | |
| 8 | |
| 9 | |
| 10 | |
| 11 | |
| 12 | |

[ Edit ]  [ Close ]

**6** Edit an unused category

**8** Close when done

**Edit**

Name  Boilers

[ OK ]  [ Cancel ]

**7** Type the name and click OK

Tip

**You can add a new product category when creating a product record.**

45

# Other Settings

There are another dozen Settings options. Have a look at them all at some point to see what's there, and note these in particular.

## Program Date

Whenever a date is required, the current date will be set as the default — though it can be easily changed. If you intend to process a lot of transactions with the same date – and not today's – set the Program Date before you start.

## Change Password

If you need to protect your accounts, you can set a password to be given at the start of every session. The password should be something you won't forget, but that others won't be able to guess easily. Ideally it should be changed regularly.

## Tax Codes

These should need no attention, but if necessary, the tax rates can be changed, or new rates entered.

## Invoice Defaults

The main thing here is to ensure that the default invoice is of the type you use most – product or service.

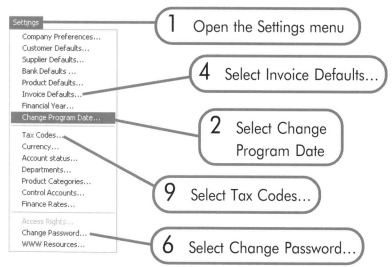

1 Open the Settings menu

4 Select Invoice Defaults...

2 Select Change Program Date

9 Select Tax Codes...

6 Select Change Password...

## Basic steps

1 Open the Settings menu.

❑ Setting the Date

2 Select Change Program Date.

3 Set the date and click OK.

❑ Invoice Defaults

4 Select Invoice Defaults...

5 Set the default format and click OK.

❑ Setting the Password

6 Select Change Password.

7 Type the password *twice* – as only asterisks are shown, this avoids mistyping errors.

8 In future, the password must be given at the start of each session.

❑ Tax Codes

9 Select Tax Codes...

10 Pick a code and click Edit

11 Enter the Description and Rate and click OK.

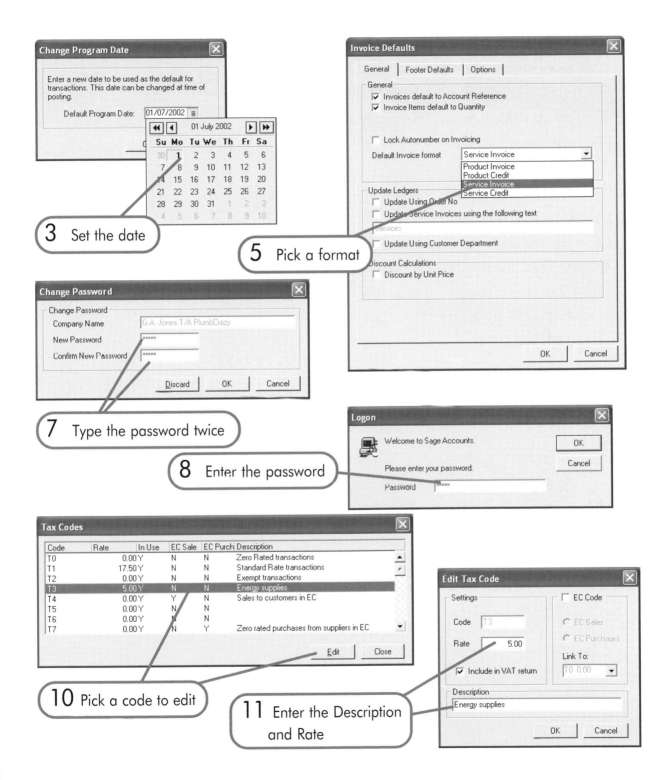

**Change Program Date**

Enter a new date to be used as the default for transactions. This date can be changed at time of posting.

Default Program Date: 01/07/2002

| | 01 July 2002 | | |
|---|---|---|---|
| Su | Mo | Tu | We | Th | Fr | Sa |
| 30 | 1 | 2 | 3 | 4 | 5 | 6 |
| 7 | 8 | 9 | 10 | 11 | 12 | 13 |
| 14 | 15 | 16 | 17 | 18 | 19 | 20 |
| 21 | 22 | 23 | 24 | 25 | 26 | 27 |
| 28 | 29 | 30 | 31 | 1 | 2 | 3 |
| 4 | 5 | 6 | 7 | 8 | 9 | 10 |

**3** Set the date

**Invoice Defaults**

General | Footer Defaults | Options

General
☑ Invoices default to Account Reference
☑ Invoice Items default to Quantity

☐ Lock Autonumber on Invoicing

Default Invoice format    Service Invoice
  Product Invoice
  Product Credit
  Service Invoice
  Service Credit

Update Ledgers
☐ Update Using Order No
☐ Update Service Invoices using the following text
  Services
☐ Update Using Customer Department

Discount Calculations
☐ Discount by Unit Price

OK    Cancel

**5** Pick a format

**Change Password**

Change Password
Company Name    G.A. Jones T/A PlumbCrazy
New Password    xxxxx
Confirm New Password    xxxxx

Discard    OK    Cancel

**7** Type the password twice

**Logon**

Welcome to Sage Accounts.

Please enter your password.

Password    xxxxx

OK    Cancel

**8** Enter the password

**Tax Codes**

| Code | Rate | In Use | EC Sale | EC Purch | Description |
|---|---|---|---|---|---|
| T0 | 0.00 | Y | N | N | Zero Rated transactions |
| T1 | 17.50 | Y | N | N | Standard Rate transactions |
| T2 | 0.00 | Y | N | N | Exempt transactions |
| T3 | 5.00 | Y | N | N | Energy supplies |
| T4 | 0.00 | Y | Y | N | Sales to customers in EC |
| T5 | 0.00 | Y | N | N | |
| T6 | 0.00 | Y | N | N | |
| T7 | 0.00 | Y | N | Y | Zero rated purchases from suppliers in EC |

Edit    Close

**10** Pick a code to edit

**Edit Tax Code**

Settings

Code    T3
Rate    5.00
☑ Include in VAT return

☐ EC Code
○ EC Sales
○ EC Purchases

Link To:
T0 0.00

Description
Energy supplies

OK    Cancel

**11** Enter the Description and Rate

# Summary

❑ The details of your business are recorded in the Company Preferences section. As with almost all of the Settings data, they can be changed at any time if necessary.

❑ If you set up defaults to suit the majority of your customers and suppliers, it will simplify life when you create new accounts.

❑ If you deal in products, you should set up suitable Product defaults.

❑ Other options on the Settings menu let you change the Program Date, Invoice defaults, Password and Tax Codes.

# 4 The Nominal Ledger

# Nominal accounts

During installation, Sage Accounts creates an extensive and well-organised set of nominal accounts, tailored to your type of business (see page 10). This may suit your needs with little or no adjustment, but can be changed easily – unwanted accounts can be deleted or their names edited, or new ones created.

The accounts most likely to need some attention are:

♦ Stock accounts (numbered from 1000), Sales (4000 onwards) and Purchases (5000 onwards) may well need renaming to suit your types of goods or services.

♦ You may want to handle computer hardware separately from other office equipment, as it can be written off in two years, rather than the standard 25% p.a. of other capital equipment. This will require two accounts, which might be named 'Computer Hardware' (or 'Computers') and 'Computer Depreciation'.

♦ Overheads (7000 onwards) should be checked to see that they agree with your categories of expenses.

♦ Some accounts may seem to be unnecessary. Don't delete any unless you are very clear about their intended use and that you do not need them. An empty account takes up a tiny amount of disk space.

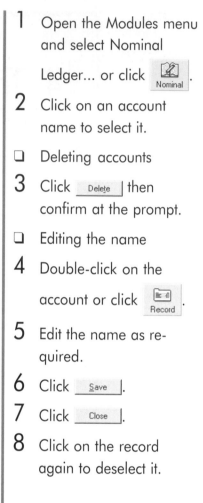

1 Open the Modules menu and select Nominal Ledger... or click [Nominal].

2 Click on an account name to select it.

❑ Deleting accounts

3 Click [Delete] then confirm at the prompt.

❑ Editing the name

4 Double-click on the account or click [Record].

5 Edit the name as required.

6 Click [Save].

7 Click [Close].

8 Click on the record again to deselect it.

## Take note

When you click Save, the details of the account disappear – don't worry about this! The panel has simply been cleared ready for work on another account. This can be selected from the list that drops down from the N/C (Nominal Code) field.

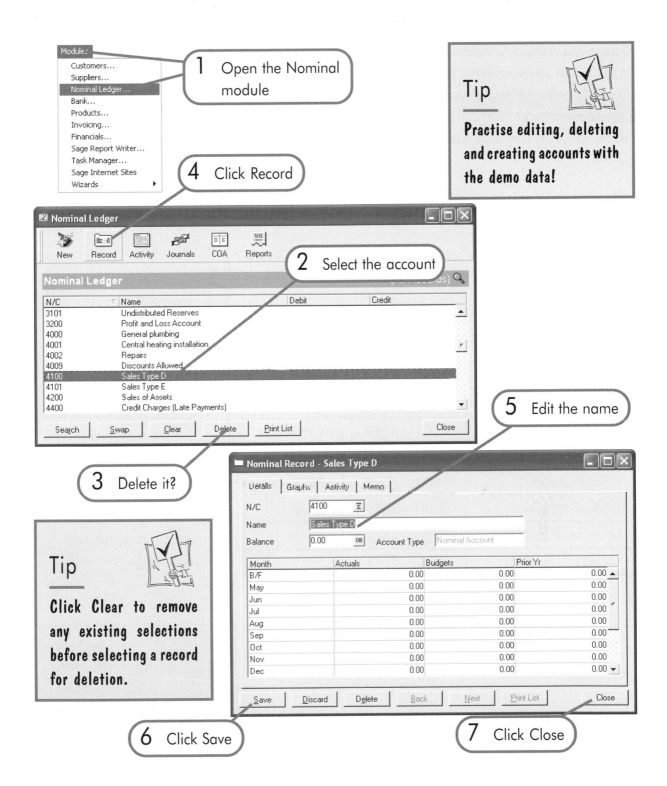

Module:
Customers...
Suppliers...
Nominal Ledger...
Bank...
Products...
Invoicing...
Financials...
Sage Report Writer...
Task Manager...
Sage Internet Sites
Wizards ▶

**1** Open the Nominal module

**Tip**

Practise editing, deleting and creating accounts with the demo data!

**4** Click Record

**Nominal Ledger**

New | Record | Activity | Journals | COA | Reports

**Nominal Ledger**

**2** Select the account

| N/C | Name | Debit | Credit |
|-----|------|-------|--------|
| 3101 | Undistributed Reserves | | |
| 3200 | Profit and Loss Account | | |
| 4000 | General plumbing | | |
| 4001 | Central heating installation | | |
| 4002 | Repairs | | |
| 4009 | Discounts Allowed | | |
| 4100 | Sales Type D | | |
| 4101 | Sales Type E | | |
| 4200 | Sales of Assets | | |
| 4400 | Credit Charges (Late Payments) | | |

Search | Swap | Clear | Delete | Print List | Close

**3** Delete it?

**5** Edit the name

**Tip**

Click Clear to remove any existing selections before selecting a record for deletion.

**Nominal Record - Sales Type D**

Details | Graphs | Activity | Memo

N/C: 4100
Name: Sales Type D
Balance: 0.00    OB    Account Type: Nominal Account

| Month | Actuals | Budgets | Prior Yr |
|-------|---------|---------|----------|
| B/F | 0.00 | 0.00 | 0.00 |
| May | 0.00 | 0.00 | 0.00 |
| Jun | 0.00 | 0.00 | 0.00 |
| Jul | 0.00 | 0.00 | 0.00 |
| Aug | 0.00 | 0.00 | 0.00 |
| Sep | 0.00 | 0.00 | 0.00 |
| Oct | 0.00 | 0.00 | 0.00 |
| Nov | 0.00 | 0.00 | 0.00 |
| Dec | 0.00 | 0.00 | 0.00 |

Save | Discard | Delete | Back | Next | Print List | Close

**6** Click Save

**7** Click Close

51

# Chart of Accounts

Before you create a new account, spend a few moments looking at the Chart of Accounts. This is used by the system when grouping and totalling accounts for calculating the Profit and Loss account (page 119) and when producing the Balance Sheet (page 120). Any new accounts must be located at an appropriate place in this structure.

The default layout is summarised below. The Initial Range shows the nominal codes currently grouped in each category type. The Maximum shows the highest code that can be included in the category type – because the next one is the first in another type.

| CATEGORY TYPE | INITIAL RANGE | MAXIMUM |
|---|---|---|
| Sales | 4000 – 4999 | |
| Purchases | 5000 – 5299 | 5999 |
| Direct Expenses | 6000 – 6299 | 6999 |
| Overheads | 7000 – 8299 | 9997 |
| Fixed assets | 0000 – 0059 | 0999 |
| Current Assets | 1000 – 1299 | 1999 |
| Current Liabilities | 2100 – 2299 | 2299 |
| Long Term Liabilities | 2300 – 2399 | 2999 |
| Capital & Reserves | 3000 – 3299 | 3999 |

Within each *Type* are *Categories*, each covering a smaller range of accounts. You can alter the ranges, to include new accounts, or add new Categories.

## Basic steps

1 In the Nominal Ledger click [D|C COA].

2 Select a Layout – at first there is only the Default.

3 Click [ Edit ].

4 Click on a Type to display its Categories.

❑ Adjusting a range

5 Type the new High code for the Category.

❑ Adding a Category

6 Type the heading.

7 Type the Low and High codes, or select them from the drop-down list.

8 Click [ Save ].

9 Close the Edit panel to return to the Chart of Accounts panel, and click [ Close ] to end.

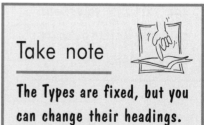

Take note

**The Types are fixed, but you can change their headings.**

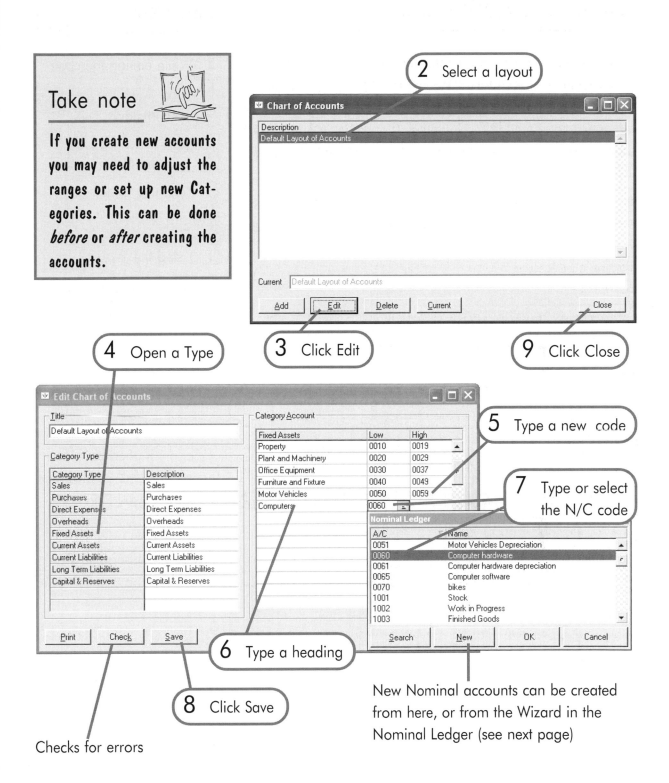

**Take note**

If you create new accounts you may need to adjust the ranges or set up new Categories. This can be done *before* or *after* creating the accounts.

**2** Select a layout

**Chart of Accounts**

Description
Default Layout of Accounts

Current   Default Layout of Accounts

Add    Edit    Delete    Current    Close

**4** Open a Type

**3** Click Edit

**9** Click Close

**Edit Chart of Accounts**

Title
Default Layout of Accounts

Category Type

| Category Type | Description |
|---|---|
| Sales | Sales |
| Purchases | Purchases |
| Direct Expenses | Direct Expenses |
| Overheads | Overheads |
| Fixed Assets | Fixed Assets |
| Current Assets | Current Assets |
| Current Liabilities | Current Liabilities |
| Long Term Liabilities | Long Term Liabilities |
| Capital & Reserves | Capital & Reserves |

Category Account

| Fixed Assets | Low | High |
|---|---|---|
| Property | 0010 | 0019 |
| Plant and Machinery | 0020 | 0029 |
| Office Equipment | 0030 | 0037 |
| Furniture and Fixture | 0040 | 0049 |
| Motor Vehicles | 0050 | 0059 |
| Computers | 0060 | |

**5** Type a new code

**7** Type or select the N/C code

**Nominal Ledger**

| A/C | Name |
|---|---|
| 0051 | Motor Vehicles Depreciation |
| 0060 | Computer hardware |
| 0061 | Computer hardware depreciation |
| 0065 | Computer software |
| 0070 | bikes |
| 1001 | Stock |
| 1002 | Work in Progress |
| 1003 | Finished Goods |

Search    New    OK    Cancel

Print    Check    Save

**6** Type a heading

**8** Click Save

Checks for errors

New Nominal accounts can be created from here, or from the Wizard in the Nominal Ledger (see next page)

# Creating a new account

When creating a new account, the key point to bear in mind is its location in the Chart of Accounts. The account must go within the range of the appropriate Type – or just outside if the range can be extended to include it. If there is an appropriate Category with unused nominal code, then that is the ideal location.

♦ New accounts can be created from within the **Edit the Chart of Accounts** panel or from the Nominal Ledger window.

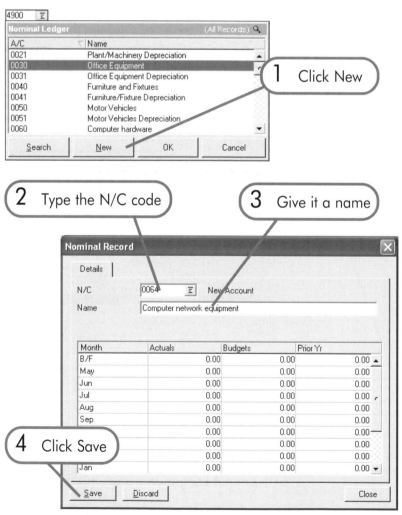

1 Click New

2 Type the N/C code

3 Give it a name

4 Click Save

# Basic steps

❑ While editing the chart

1 Drop down the list of accounts and click 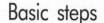.

2 Type the N/C number.

3 Type the Name.

4 Click Save.

❑ Using the Wizard

5 In the Nominal Ledger window, click .

6 Enter the Name and select the Type.

*Either*

7 Select a suitable Category if possible – the account will be given the next unused Refn code.

*Or*

8 Select (Un-named Category) and type the Refn code.

9 The opening balance can be entered now if you like (see page 56).

**Nominal Record Wizard**

Nominal Information

**Entering your nominal code name and type.**

To create a new nominal account, you need to enter the nominal account's name and select the type of nominal account that you are creating.

Name    Computer software

Type    Sales

Overheads
Fixed Assets
Current Assets
Current Liabilities

Cancel        Back    Next    Finish

**Nominal Record Wizard**

Nominal Information

**Entering your nominal category and account code.**

The new nominal account can be given a category within the chart of accounts and a unique reference code to identify the account.

Category    [Un-named category]

Refn    0060

Cancel        Back    Next    Finish

**6**  Give it a Name and pick the Type

**8**  Select Un-named and type the N/C code

**9**  Enter the opening balance?

al Record Wiz

Nominal Information

**Choosing to enter your nominal account's opening balance.**

Do you wish to post an opening balance for your new nominal account?

( ) No, there is no opening balance to enter.
( ) Yes, I wish to enter an opening balance.

Cancel        Back    Next    Finish

# Opening balances

When you transfer to the Sage system, opening balances (O/B) should normally be entered on all accounts where transactions have taken place. In an ongoing business this will probably mean all used accounts, except those of suppliers and customers where debts have been cleared. If the business is just being started up, you will still need to enter opening balances in the Capital and Bank accounts, and perhaps in those for property and other assets.

Opening balances may also be needed when you create new accounts. This is less likely with customers and suppliers, where you will normally set up the account with a zero balance before you begin to record your transactions.

This is one of the few occasions where you have to do the double-entry bookkeeping yourself. Every opening balance must have an equivalent entry in another account – every debit needs a balancing credit, and vice versa. Remember:

♦ **Debit**: movement of value into an account.

♦ **Credit**: movement of value out of an account.

e.g. when you have bought something it will be entered as a Debit in the apropriate asset, purchase or expense account and a Credit in a bank or supplier's account.

❑ Existing accounts

1 Select the record(s) to be edited.

2 Click .

3 In the Balance field, click ⊡.

4 Set the Date.

5 Enter the value into the Debit or Credit field.

6 Click Save.

❑ If several records have been selected, click Next to go to the next, and repeat steps 3 to 6.

7 Enter the balancing values into the appropriate accounts.

8 Click Close.

❑ New accounts

9 At the third stage of the Wizard, select or enter an opening balance, then enter the Date and Amount, and select Debit or Credit.

---

## Tip

If the balancing entry is omitted, mistyped or posted to the 'wrong side', it will be recorded in the Suspense Account (Nominal Code 9998). Check this after you have entered any opening balances. Mispostings can be corrected by Journal entries (see page 64).

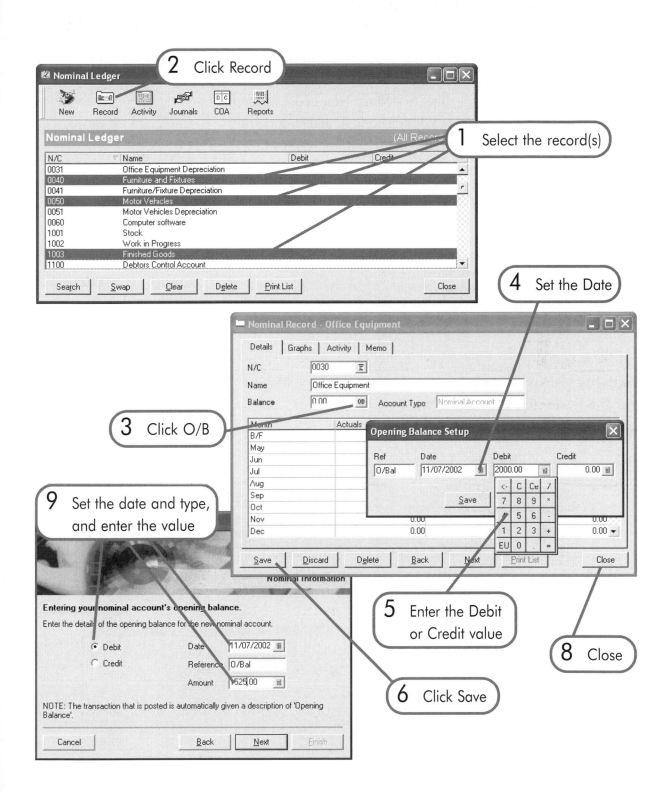

**2** Click Record

**Nominal Ledger**

New  Record  Activity  Journals  COA  Reports

**Nominal Ledger** (All Record

**1** Select the record(s)

| N/C | Name | Debit | Credit |
|------|------|-------|--------|
| 0031 | Office Equipment Depreciation | | |
| 0040 | Furniture and Fixtures | | |
| 0041 | Furniture/Fixture Depreciation | | |
| 0050 | Motor Vehicles | | |
| 0051 | Motor Vehicles Depreciation | | |
| 0060 | Computer software | | |
| 1001 | Stock | | |
| 1002 | Work in Progress | | |
| 1003 | Finished Goods | | |
| 1100 | Debtors Control Account | | |

Search   Swap   Clear   Delete   Print List   Close

**4** Set the Date

**Nominal Record - Office Equipment**

Details | Graphs | Activity | Memo

N/C       0030
Name      Office Equipment
Balance   0.00   OB   Account Type   Nominal Account

**3** Click O/B

| Month | Actuals |
|-------|---------|
| B/F | |
| May | |
| Jun | |
| Jul | |
| Aug | |
| Sep | |
| Oct | |
| Nov | 0.00 |
| Dec | 0.00 |

**Opening Balance Setup**

Ref     Date         Debit       Credit
O/Bal   11/07/2002   2000.00     0.00

Save

<- | C | Ce | /
7 | 8 | 9 | x
4 | 5 | 6 | -
1 | 2 | 3 | +
EU | 0 | . | =

0.00
0.00

Save   Discard   Delete   Back   Next   Print List   Close

**9** Set the date and type, and enter the value

**Nominal Information**

**Entering your nominal account's opening balance.**

Enter the details of the opening balance for the new nominal account.

⦿ Debit        Date        11/07/2002
○ Credit       Reference   O/Bal
               Amount      525.00

NOTE: The transaction that is posted is automatically given a description of 'Opening Balance'.

Cancel        Back   Next   Finish

**5** Enter the Debit or Credit value

**8** Close

**6** Click Save

57

# Nominal records

Though the Nominal Ledger is the heart of the accounting system, once it is set up there are relatively few situations in which you will work on it directly. Most Nominal Ledger entries arise from transactions with customers and suppliers, which are normally handled through the Invoicing (Chapter 6), Bank (Chapter 7), Customers or Suppliers (Chapter 5) modules.

The Nominal module is mainly used for viewing Nominal records, for performing (fairly rare) journal entries, and for setting up budgets.

The record panels have four tabs:

**Details**    shows the current balance, and the balance, budget and prior year figures for each month (if available).

**Graphs**    shows the same monthly figures in visual form.

**Activity**    shows the transactions currently in the audit trail for that account.

**Memo**    is a free space in which any notes can be written.

## Basic steps

❑ Viewing records

1 Click  to open the Nominal Ledger module.

2 Select the record(s).

3 Click [Record] .

4 Click on the headings to switch between the tabs.

5 Click [ Next ] to view the next record.

6 Click [ Close ] when done.

The current balances are displayed here

( 3 Click Record )

( 2 Select the record(s) )

**Nominal Ledger**

New   Record   Activity   Journals   COA   Reports

Nominal Ledger                                            (All Records)

| N/C | Name | Debit | Credit |
|-----|------|-------|--------|
| 1100 | Debtors Control Account | | 31570.47 |
| 1101 | Sundry Debtors | | |
| 1102 | Other Debtors | | |
| 1103 | Prepayments | | |
| 1200 | Bank Current Account | 39346.79 | |
| 1210 | Bank Deposit Account | 3510.00 | |
| 1220 | Building Society Account | 507.53 | |
| 1230 | Petty Cash | 1130.48 | |
| 1240 | Company Credit Card | 9358.97 | |
| 2100 | Creditors Control Account | | 41194.76 |

Use Search to filter the records in the list

Search   Swap   Clear   Delete   Print List                    Close

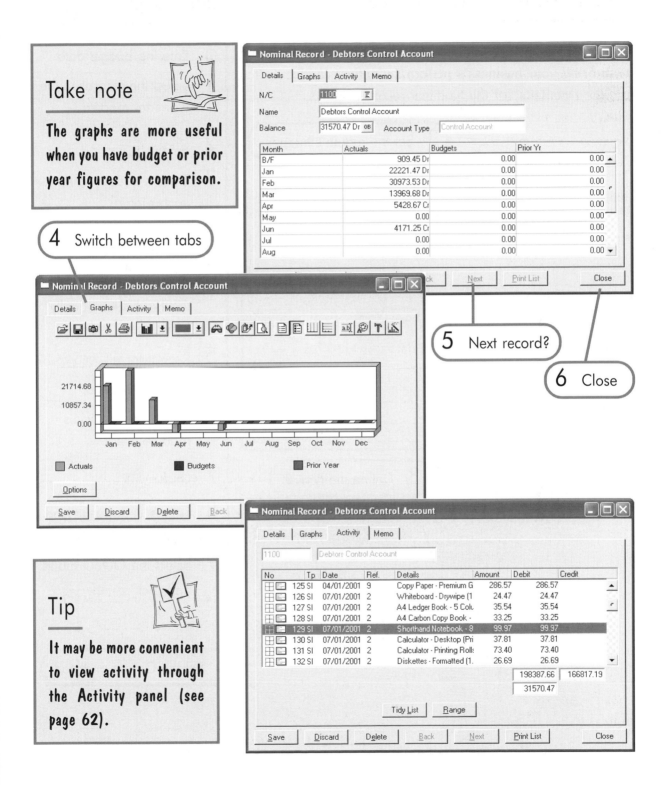

## Take note

The graphs are more useful when you have budget or prior year figures for comparison.

**4** Switch between tabs

**5** Next record?

**6** Close

## Tip

It may be more convenient to view activity through the Activity panel (see page 62).

# Budget

If you want to include budget figures to help in analysing and monitoring your business's performance, they can be written into the Details tab of the Nominal record displays.

## Basic steps

❏ Entering budget data

1 Select the records in the Nominal module.

2 Click .

3 Enter a budget figure for each month.

*Or*

4 Enter a figure for the year in the Total row. It will be divided equally between the months.

5 Repeat for all records.

❏ The Budget report

6 Open the Financials module window.

7 Click 🖼.

8 Set the Period start and end.

9 Select the Output mode and click OK .

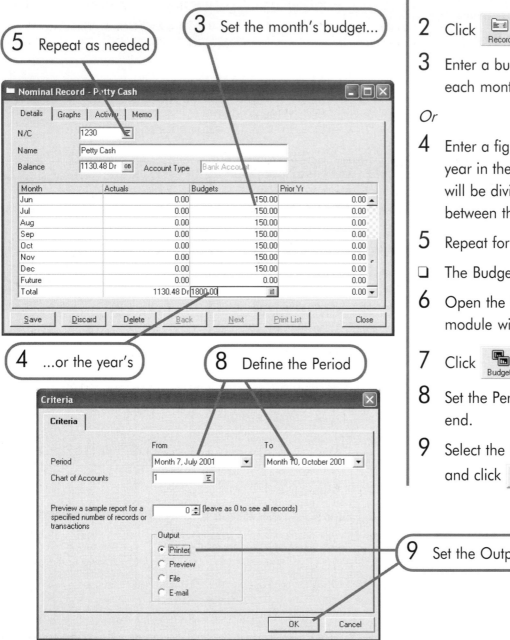

**5** Repeat as needed

**3** Set the month's budget...

**Nominal Record - Petty Cash**

Details | Graphs | Activity | Memo

N/C 1230

Name Petty Cash

Balance 1130.48 Dr OB  Account Type Bank Account

| Month | Actuals | Budgets | Prior Yr |
|---|---|---|---|
| Jun | 0.00 | 150.00 | 0.00 |
| Jul | 0.00 | 150.00 | 0.00 |
| Aug | 0.00 | 150.00 | 0.00 |
| Sep | 0.00 | 150.00 | 0.00 |
| Oct | 0.00 | 150.00 | 0.00 |
| Nov | 0.00 | 150.00 | 0.00 |
| Dec | 0.00 | 150.00 | 0.00 |
| Future | 0.00 | 0.00 | 0.00 |
| Total | 1130.48 Dr | 1800.00 | 0.00 |

Save | Discard | Delete | Back | Next | Print List | Close

**4** ...or the year's

**8** Define the Period

**Criteria**

Criteria

| | From | To |
|---|---|---|
| Period | Month 7, July 2001 | Month 10, October 2001 |
| Chart of Accounts | 1 | |

Preview a sample report for a specified number of records or transactions: 0 (leave as 0 to see all records)

Output
- ⊙ Printer
- ○ Preview
- ○ File
- ○ E-mail

OK | Cancel

**9** Set the Output and start

# Budget report

This report, produced in the Financials module, shows how far your actual figures differ from the budget, for the period and for the year to date. It also shows, in the Ratio(%) columns, the relative contribution of each category of sales to the total income, and of each category of expenditure to the total costs.

**Date:** 11/07/2002
**Time:** 15:35:52

**Page:** 1

### G.A. Jones T/A PlumbCrazy
### Budget Report

**From:** Month 7, July 2002
**To:** Month 10, October 2002

**Chart of Accounts:**         Default Layout of Accounts

| | Actual | Ratio(%) | Period Budget | Variance | Actual | Ratio(%) | Year to Date Budget | Variance |
|---|---|---|---|---|---|---|---|---|
| **Sales** | | | | | | | | |
| Product Sales | 10,659.00 | 76.67 | 15,000.00 | (4,341.00) | 12,574.00 | 79.50 | 22,500.00 | (9,926.00) |
| Other Sales | 3,243.30 | 23.33 | 2,000.00 | 1,243.30 | 3,243.30 | 20.50 | 3,000.00 | 243.30 |
| | 13,902.30 | 100.00 | 17,000.00 | (3,097.70) | 15,817.30 | 100.00 | 25,500.00 | (9,682.70) |
| **Purchases** | | | | | | | | |
| Consumables Purchases | 2,976.00 | 21.41 | 3,000.00 | (24.00) | 2,976.00 | 18.81 | 4,500.00 | (1,524.00) |
| Stock | 1,800.00 | 12.95 | 0.00 | 1,800.00 | 1,800.00 | 11.38 | 0.00 | 1,800.00 |
| | 4,776.00 | 34.35 | 3,000.00 | 1,776.00 | 4,776.00 | 30.19 | 4,500.00 | 276.00 |
| **Direct Expenses** | | | | | | | | |
| | 0.00 | 0.00 | 0.00 | 0.00 | 0.00 | 0.00 | 0.00 | 0.00 |
| **Gross Profit/(Loss):** | 9,126.30 | 65.65 | 14,000.00 | (4,873.70) | 11,041.30 | 69.81 | 21,000.00 | (9,958.70) |
| **Overheads** | | | | | | | | |
| Rent and Rates | 1,080.00 | 7.77 | 1,333.32 | (253.32) | 1,080.00 | 6.83 | 1,999.98 | (919.98) |
| Heat, Light and Power | 203.00 | 1.46 | 150.00 | 53.00 | 571.00 | 3.61 | 450.00 | 121.00 |
| Motor Expenses | 853.61 | 6.14 | 1,200.00 | (346.39) | 853.61 | 5.40 | 1,800.00 | (946.39) |
| Printing and Stationery | 17.50 | 0.13 | 80.00 | (62.50) | 17.50 | 0.11 | 120.00 | (102.50) |
| Depreciation | 1,500.00 | 10.79 | 1,000.00 | 500.00 | 1,500.00 | 9.48 | 1,000.00 | 500.00 |
| General Expenses | 0.10 | 0.00 | 400.00 | (399.90) | 0.10 | 0.00 | 600.00 | (599.90) |
| Suspense & Mispostings | (0.10) | (0.00) | 0.00 | (0.10) | (0.10) | (0.00) | 0.00 | (0.10) |
| | 3,654.11 | 26.28 | 4,163.32 | (509.21) | 4,022.11 | 25.43 | 5,969.98 | (1,947.87) |
| **Net Profit/(Loss):** | 5,472.19 | 39.36 | 9,836.68 | (4,364.49) | 7,019.19 | 44.38 | 15,030.02 | (8,010.83) |

End of Report

# Activity

If your main interest is in the transactions in the Nominal accounts, you may prefer to view them through the Activity display. The same information is shown as in the Activity tab of the record panel, but you can move more easily between different records here.

When using this panel, you may find it useful to set the Criteria to filter the list so you only see those types of records that you are interested in at the time. The Criteria can be set from the Nominal window, or from within the drop-down list of records.

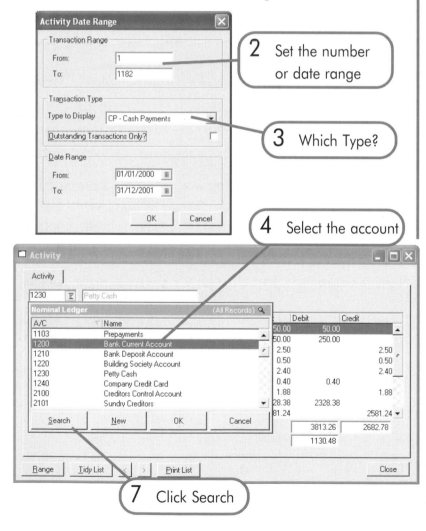

**2** Set the number or date range

**3** Which Type?

**4** Select the account

**7** Click Search

1 Click .

2 Set the range by selecting numbers or dates.

3 Select a Transaction Type if required.

4 Select an account from the drop-down list.

5 Click ⬚ if you want details of a transaction.

6 Use ▷ to view the next record, or select another from the account list.

❑ Setting Criteria

7 Click .

8 Select *Where* in the Join column.

9 Select a Field then set the Condition and Value.

10 Click .

---

Tip

The default date range is 1980 to 2099. It is quicker to type the dates than set them with the calendar!

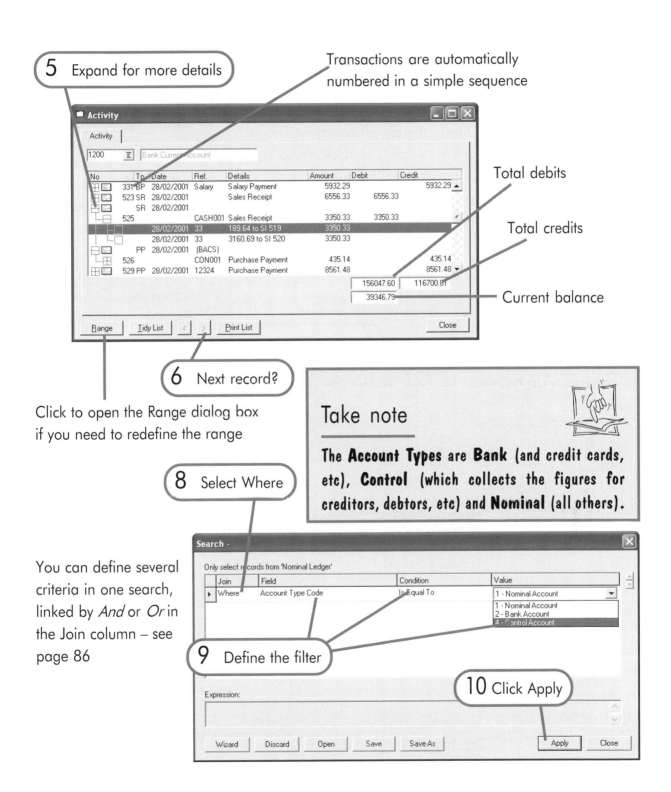

**5** Expand for more details

Transactions are automatically numbered in a simple sequence

**Activity**

Activity

1200  Bank Current Account

| No | Tp | Date | Ref. | Details | Amount | Debit | Credit |
|----|----|------|------|---------|--------|-------|--------|
| 331 | BP | 28/02/2001 | Salary | Salary Payment | 5932.29 | | 5932.29 |
| 523 | SR | 28/02/2001 | | Sales Receipt | 6556.33 | 6556.33 | |
| | SR | 28/02/2001 | | | | | |
| 525 | | | CASH001 | Sales Receipt | 3350.33 | 3350.33 | |
| | | 28/02/2001 | 33 | 189.64 to SI 519 | 3350.33 | | |
| | | 28/02/2001 | 33 | 3160.69 to SI 520 | 3350.33 | | |
| | PP | 28/02/2001 | (BACS) | | | | |
| 526 | | | CON001 | Purchase Payment | 435.14 | | 435.14 |
| 529 | PP | 28/02/2001 | 12324 | Purchase Payment | 8561.48 | | 8561.48 |

Total debits

Total credits

|  | 156047.60 | 116700.81 |
|--|-----------|-----------|
|  | 39346.79 | |

Current balance

Range | Tidy List | < | > | Print List | Close

**6** Next record?

Click to open the Range dialog box if you need to redefine the range

**8** Select Where

**Take note**

The **Account Types** are **Bank** (and credit cards, etc), **Control** (which collects the figures for creditors, debtors, etc) and **Nominal** (all others).

You can define several criteria in one search, linked by *And* or *Or* in the Join column – see page 86

**9** Define the filter

**10** Click Apply

**Search -**

Only select records from 'Nominal Ledger'

| Join | Field | Condition | Value |
|------|-------|-----------|-------|
| Where | Account Type Code | Is Equal To | 1 - Nominal Account |
| | | | 1 - Nominal Account |
| | | | 2 - Bank Account |
| | | | 4 - Control Account |

Expression:

Wizard | Discard | Open | Save | Save As | Apply | Close

63

# Journals

A journal entry is a transfer between Nominal accounts. Typical uses include recording depreciation or the revaluation of stock or other assets.

Making a journal entry is one of the few situations where you have to do the double-entry bookkeeping yourself, rather than leaving it to the system. An entry normally consists of a pair of transactions, one debit, one credit. Sometimes there will be more than two, but the total debits and credits must always balance — you cannot save the entries until it does!

## Basic steps

1   Click .

2   Give a Ref code to identify the journal.

3   Set the Date.

4   Set the N/C number of the Nominal account.

5   Type the Details.

6   Enter the Debit or Credit.

7   Repeat steps 4 to 6 for the other transaction(s).

8   Click $\underline{S}$ave .

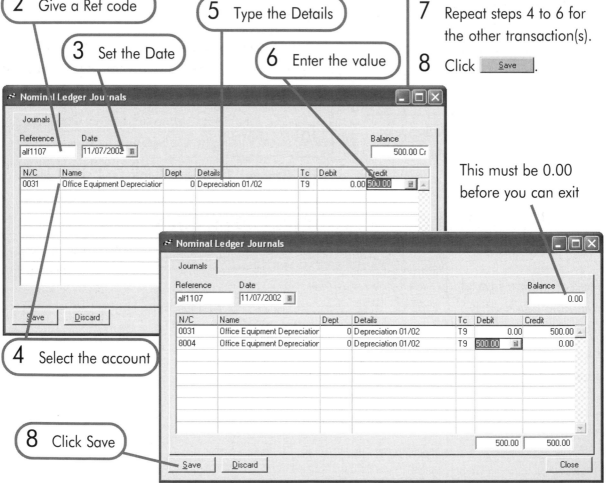

2   Give a Ref code

3   Set the Date

5   Type the Details

6   Enter the value

4   Select the account

8   Click Save

This must be 0.00 before you can exit

# Detour: depreciation

## Tip

For fast-depreciating items such as computers and cars, it may be better to work from second-hand market values, or write off the value according to the Inland Revenue's rules for Capital Allowances.

The purpose of depreciation is to ensure that the values of assets are recorded realistically in the accounts.

There are several ways to calculate it, of which the simplest is the 'Straight Line' method. To do this, work out the difference between the original cost and its residual value at the end of its useful life, then divide by the years. For example, a display cabinet costing £1,200 may have an estimated life of around 4 years, and a residual value of £200. That gives you (£1200 – £200) / 4 = £250 annual depreciation.

However you calculate it, depreciation should be recorded by the journal entries:

♦ a *Credit* in the depreciation account in the Fixed Asset area (Nominal codes 0000 to 0099), reducing the value of the asset;

♦ a *Debit* in the equivalent account in the Depreciation section of the Overheads area (Nominal codes 8000 to 8099), reducing the net profit and hence the total capital of the business.

## Edit Chart of Accounts

**Title**

Default Layout of Accounts

**Category Type**

| Category Type | Description |
|---|---|
| Sales | Sales |
| Purchases | Purchases |
| Direct Expenses | Direct Expenses |
| Overheads | Overheads |
| Fixed Assets | Fixed Assets |
| Current Assets | Current Assets |
| Current Liabilities | Current Liabilities |
| Long Term Liabilities | Long Term Liabilities |
| Capital & Reserves | Capital & Reserves |

**Category Account**

| Overheads | Low | High |
|---|---|---|
| Rent and Rates | 7100 | 7199 |
| Heat, Light and Power | 7200 | 7299 |
| Motor Expenses | 7300 | 7399 |
| Travelling and Entertainment | 7400 | 7499 |
| Printing and Stationery | 7500 | 7599 |
| Professional Fees | 7600 | 7699 |
| Equipment Hire and Rental | 7700 | 7799 |
| Maintenance | 7800 | 7899 |
| Bank Charges and Interest | 7900 | 7999 |
| Depreciation | 8000 | 8099 |
| Bad Debts | 8100 | 8199 |
| General Expenses | 8200 | 8299 |
| Suspense & Mispostings | 9998 | 9999 |

Print    Check    Save                                    Close

The Fixed Asset, Depreciation and Overheads areas and sections referred to above relate to the Chart of Accounts (see page 52).

Click [COA] in the Nominal window to open it.

# Reports

Five types of reports are available in the Nominal module.

♦ **Day Books:** Lists transactions in numeric order;

♦ **Nominal Activity**: Groups transactions by their Nominal accounts;

♦ **Nominal Balances**: Lists the balance in each account;

♦ **Nominal List**: A simple list of Nominal accounts;

♦ **Nominal Record CSV**: Lists the accounts and their monthly budget in Comma Separated Values format. This is a standard format, recognised by most databases and spreadsheets, and should be used if you want to process the data further using one of these applications.

The last report always lists all the transactions (or at least, all those not yet cleared from the audit trail, see page 114). The other four can list all or a selected range. Depending upon the type of report, this can be based on the nominal code, date, transaction number or department.

see page 114

## Basic steps

1 Click .

2 Select a layout.

3 Choose the Output – Printer, Preview, File or E-mail.

4 Click Run .

5 To restrict the range, set Nominal Code limits in the Criteria dialog box and click OK .

6 If you are previewing, use the buttons to Print, if desired.

7 Click Close .

## Take note

If you select a report and click Edit, it is taken into the Report Designer (see page 82).

see page 82

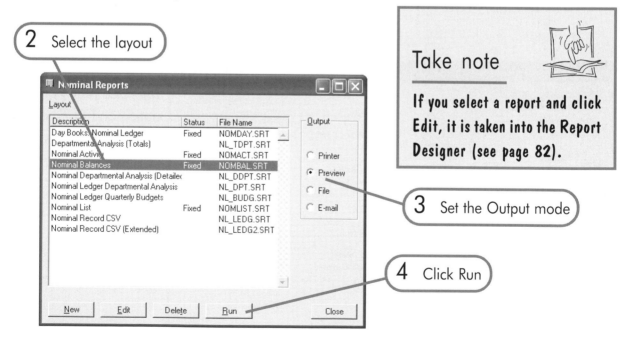

2 Select the layout

3 Set the Output mode

4 Click Run

**Nominal Reports**

Layout

| Description | Status | File Name |
|---|---|---|
| Day Books: Nominal Ledger | Fixed | NOMDAY.SRT |
| Departmental Analysis (Totals) | | NL_TDPT.SRT |
| Nominal Activity | Fixed | NOMACT.SRT |
| Nominal Balances | Fixed | NOMBAL.SRT |
| Nominal Departmental Analysis (Detailed | | NL_DDPT.SRT |
| Nominal Ledger Departmental Analysis | | NL_DPT.SRT |
| Nominal Ledger Quarterly Budgets | | NL_BUDG.SRT |
| Nominal List | Fixed | NOMLIST.SRT |
| Nominal Record CSV | | NL_LEDG.SRT |
| Nominal Record CSV (Extended) | | NL_LEDG2.SRT |

Output

○ Printer
● Preview
○ File
○ E-mail

New   Edit   Delete   Run   Close

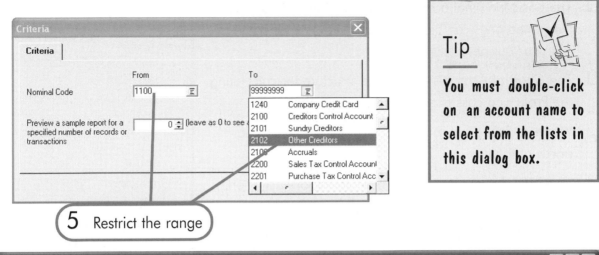

5    Restrict the range

**Sage Line 50 Accountant - G.A. Jones T/A PlumbCrazy - [NOMBAL.SRT]**

File   Edit   View   Modules   Settings   Tools   Favourites   Window   Help

Customers   Suppliers   Nominal   Bank   Products   Invoicing   Financials   Period End   Reports   Tasks   sage.com   Help

**Date:**   11/07/2002        G.A. Jones T/A PlumbCrazy        **Page:**   1
**Time:**   17:54:58        Nominal Balances

**N/C From:**   1100
**N/C To:**   2102

| N/C | Name | Debit | Credit |
|---|---|---|---|
| 1100 | Debtors Control Account | 31,570.47 | |
| 1101 | Sundry Debtors | | |
| 1102 | Other Debtors | | |
| 1103 | Prepayments | | |
| 1200 | Bank Current Account | 39,346.79 | |
| 1210 | Bank Deposit Account | 3,510.00 | |
| 1220 | Building Society Account | 507.53 | |
| 1230 | Petty Cash | 1,130.48 | |
| 1240 | Company Credit Card | 9,358.97 | |
| 2100 | Creditors Control Account | | 41,194.76 |
| 2101 | Sundry Creditors | | |
| 2102 | Other Creditors | | |
| | | 85,424.24 | 41,194.76 |

End of Report

Open   Save As   E-mail   Page Setup   Print Setup   Print   Styles   Zoom   Close

Page 1/1

6   Print?               7   Click Close

# Summary

- [ ] The basic Nominal accounts have been created for you. Unwanted ones can be deleted and new ones created to suit your business.

- [ ] The Chart of Accounts creates the structure for calculating the Profit and Loss account and Balance Sheet.

- [ ] When you set up accounts, you can enter opening balances at the time.

- [ ] If wanted, budget figures can be entered for each month in Nominal accounts. Comparing these with actual figures can be instructive.

- [ ] The Activity tab offers the best way to view Nominal account transactions.

- [ ] Journal entries are used to transfer value between Nominal accounts. Recording depreciation is a typical use for them.

- [ ] The reports available from the Nominal module include simple and grouped lists of transactions and summaries of account balances.

# 5 Customers/suppliers

# The New Wizard

Within the Sage systems, customers and suppliers are handled in almost identical ways, as you might expect – the trading relationship is the same, but viewed from opposite ends. The examples in this chapter are all drawn from the Customer module, but – with rare exceptions – could just as well have come from the Suppliers.

New accounts can be set up from the New button in the list of accounts in the invoicing, receipts and payments windows – a blank record opens to receive the details. However, the simplest way to set up an account is to use the New Wizard in the Customer and Supplier modules. This helps to ensure that all the essential information is entered, and creates the Refn (reference) code from the customer/supplier name.

**1** Open the Customer module window and click .

**2** Enter the Name. A Refn will be generated – edit this to make it easier to recognise, if necessary.

**3** Enter the Address details.

**4** Enter the Contact details.

**5** Set the Account Status – normally Open (active, existing client) or New.

**6** At the three Additional Information stages, check and adjust the Credit Limit and Terms as required.

**7** If you are bringing an existing customer onto the system, you may need to set the opening balance.

---

**Customer Record Wizard**

Customer Information

**Entering your Customer's name and unique reference.**

To create a new customer account you need to enter the customer's name and a unique reference.

Name    Plumpton Institute

Refn    PLUMPINS

Cancel        Back        Next        Finish

**2** Enter the Name and edit the Refn

Click Next after each stage

---

## Tip

**Missing details can be entered into the record at any time.**

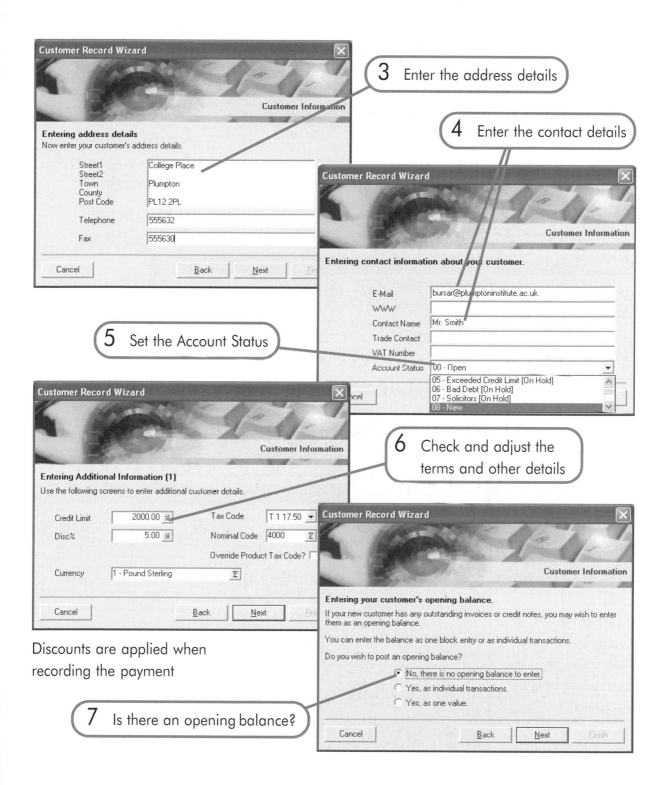

**3** Enter the address details

**4** Enter the contact details

**Customer Record Wizard**

Customer Information

**Entering address details**
Now enter your customer's address details.

| | |
|---|---|
| Street1 | College Place |
| Street2 | |
| Town | Plumpton |
| County | |
| Post Code | PL12 2PL |
| Telephone | 555632 |
| Fax | 555630 |

Cancel    Back    Next    Fini

**Customer Record Wizard**

Customer Information

**Entering contact information about your customer.**

| | |
|---|---|
| E-Mail | bursar@plumptoninstitute.ac.uk |
| WWW | |
| Contact Name | Mr. Smith |
| Trade Contact | |
| VAT Number | |
| Account Status | 00 - Open |

05 - Exceeded Credit Limit [On Hold]
06 - Bad Debt [On Hold]
07 - Solicitors [On Hold]
08 - New

**5** Set the Account Status

**Customer Record Wizard**

Customer Information

**Entering Additional Information (1)**
Use the following screens to enter additional customer details.

| | | | |
|---|---|---|---|
| Credit Limit | 2000.00 | Tax Code | T 1 17.50 |
| Disc% | 5.00 | Nominal Code | 4000 |
| | | Override Product Tax Code? | |
| Currency | 1 - Pound Sterling | | |

Cancel    Back    Next    Fini

Discounts are applied when
recording the payment

**6** Check and adjust the
terms and other details

**Customer Record Wizard**

Customer Information

**Entering your customer's opening balance.**
If your new customer has any outstanding invoices or credit notes, you may wish to enter them as an opening balance.

You can enter the balance as one block entry or as individual transactions.

Do you wish to post an opening balance?

- ● No, there is no opening balance to enter.
- ○ Yes, as individual transactions.
- ○ Yes, as one value.

Cancel    Back    Next    Finish

**7** Is there an opening balance?

# Editing records

The record displays for customers and suppliers show not simply their contact details and terms of trade, but also the flow of business to date and the current state of their accounts.

◆ You can edit the information on the Details, Defaults and Memo tabs. The rest are for display only.

1 Select the record(s) you want to view or edit.

2 Click ▭Record.

3 Add the Contact name and VAT number to the Details, if relevant.

4 Switch to Defaults to check the settings.

**2 Click Record**

**1 Select the record(s)**

## Customers

New | Record | Activity | Aged | Invoice | Credit | Charges | Phone | Labels | Letters | Statement | Reports

### Customers
(All Records)

| A/C | Name | Balance | Crd Limit | Contact |
|-----|------|---------|-----------|---------|
| JONESG | Mr G. Jones | 58.16 | 500.00 | |
| JONESJ | Ms J. Jones | 0.00 | 500.00 | |
| PLUMPINS | Plumpton Institute | 0.00 | 2000.00 | Mr. Smith |
| PLUMPTC | Plumpton Town Council | 437.34 | 5000.00 | |
| REVGREEN | Rev Green | 75.81 | 500.00 | |
| RIBBONS | Ribbons and Bows | 362.50 | 500.00 | Mrs Perkins |
| SMITH01 | Mr & Mrs I Smith | 0.00 | 500.00 | |
| WHITE | Mrs E. White | 425.00 | 500.00 | |

Search | Swap | Clear | Delete | Print List | Close

## Customer - Plumpton Town Council

Details | Defaults | Credit Control | Sales | Graphs | Activity | Memo

**3 Any Details to add?**

If you make any changes, click Save before you go to the next record or close the panel.

### Account Details
A/C: PLUMPTC
Name: Plumpton Town Council

### Status
Balance: 5342.66 OB
Acc.Status: 0 Open

### Address
Street1: Town Hall
Street2: Main Street
Town: Plumpton
County:
Post Code:
VAT Number:

### Contact Information
Contact name:
Trade contact:
Telephone: 555010
Telephone 2:
Fax: 555020
E-Mail:
WWW:

Save | Discard | Delete | Back | Next | Print List | Close

# The Sales tab

❑ Viewing Sales

**5** Switch to the Sales tab.

**6** Double-click on a cell for its details panel.

**7** Click on ⊞ to open up any item.

**8** Click Close .

This displays a summary of the invoices, credits, balances and receipts for each month in the current year.

**5** Click to open the Sales tab

Check the top-line fields for a snapshot of the trading position

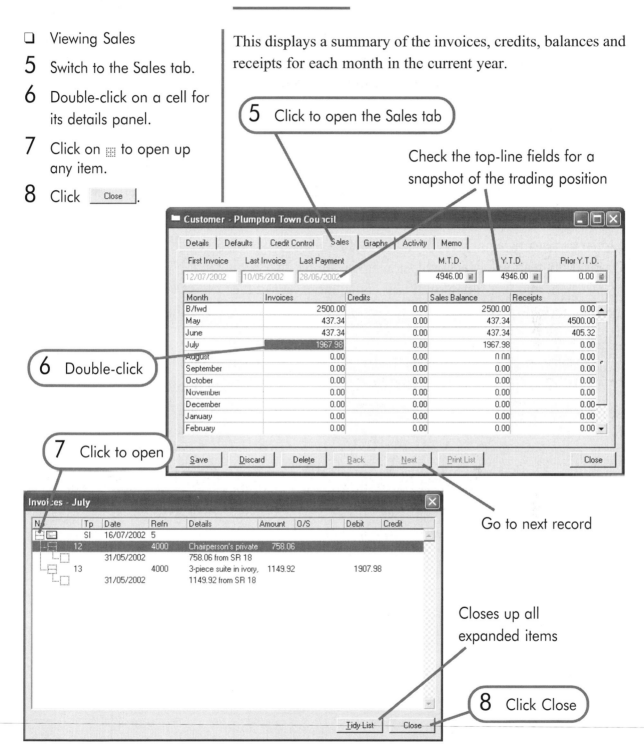

**6** Double-click

**7** Click to open

Go to next record

Closes up all expanded items

**8** Click Close

# Graphs

Graphs can help to show underlying trends that are not immediately visible from the raw data. With the right sort of graph – bar chart, pie chart, line, scatter or Hi-Lo graph – presented in the right way, you can see relationships and changes over time, much more clearly than you can by poring over sets of numbers. On the other hand, you can spend an awful lot of time trying out different display modes and tweaking the layout and design – and not have much to show for it at the end of the day.

I suspect that, in most firms, the trading patterns with their regular customers/suppliers will follow fairly simple trends or seasonal fluctuations, which will show up on simple line, area or bar chart, and that little useful will come out of any of the more esoteric display modes.

**Tip**

If you want to use the graphs productively, spend an hour one day playing with the settings until you are happy with them – then leave them alone. These settings will become the defaults for all future graphs.

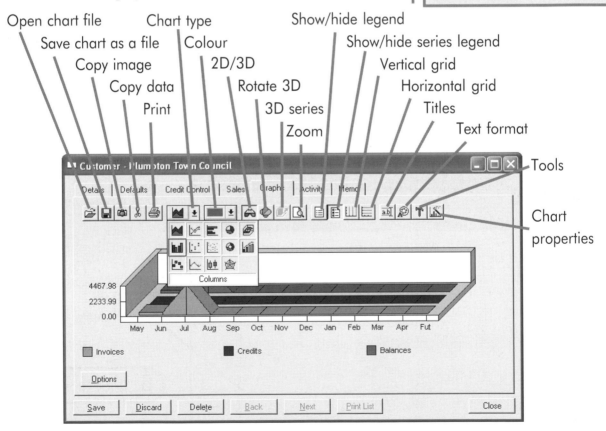

74

## Basic steps

1  Switch to the Graphs tab.

2  Select a type.

3  Experiment with the tools to see what they do and find settings that you like.

*and/or*

4  Open the Properties panel, experiment and set the options there.

---

## Tip

The Copy data tool ✂ copies the graph's figures to the Clipboard as text. They can then be pasted into a word-processor.

The Copy image tool 📷 captures the graph as a picture. Paste it into a graphics application.

---

1  Switch to Graphs

2  Select the type

3  Use the tools

**Customer - Plumpton Town Council**

Details | Defaults | Credit Control | Sales | Graphs | Activity | Memo

4467.98
2233.99
0.00
May Jun Jul Aug Sep Oct Nov Dec Jan Feb Mar Apr Fut

☐ Invoices          ■ Credits          ■ Balances

Options

Save | Discard | Delete | Back | Next | Print List | Close

4  Open the Chart Properties panel

Use the Series tab to format each series (set of figures) separately

**Chart properties**

General | Series | Scale | 3D View | Titles

Drag the buttons to rotate the image

X Angle: 45
Y Angle: 20

☑ 3D
☑ Full 3D View
☑ Shadows

Click Apply to test a setting without closing the panel

Apply | OK | Cancel

# The Activity tab

This lists all the transactions to date, back to the point when the audit trail was last cleared (see page 120). It also shows the total amounts outstanding in each Aged period.

A busy account can produce a long list of transactions. If you don't want to struggle through the list – and scrolling is distinctly jerky in these displays – use the Range button to restrict the display to a selected set of transactions.

## Basic steps

1 Switch to the Activity tab.

2 Click ▦ to see the details of an item.

3 Use [ Tidy List ] to close up all expanded items.

4 Click [ Range ] then set the numbers or dates to restrict the range.

**2 Expand an item**

**1 Switch to Activity**

**Customer   Plumpton Town Council**

| Details | Defaults | Credit Control | Sales | Graphs | Activity | Memo |

| A/C | PLUMPTC | | Balance | 437.34 |
| Name | Plumpton Town Council | | Amount Paid | 4905.32 |
| Credit Limit | 5000.00 | | Turnover YTD | 4946.00 |

| No | Tp | Date | Refn | Details | Amount | O/S | Debit | Credit |
|----|----|------|------|---------|--------|-----|-------|--------|
| ▦ | SI | 16/07/2002 | 5 | | | | | |
| | 12 | | 4000 | Chairperson's private | 758.06 | | | |
| | 13 | | 4000 | 3-piece suite in ivory, | 1149.92 | | 1907.98 | |
| | | 31/05/2002 | | 1149.92 from SR 18 | | | | |
| ▦ | 14 SI | 14/06/2002 | 4 | Annual Boiler Service | 437.34 | | 437.34 | |

**3 Close up all expanded items**

| Future | Current | 30 Days | 60 Days | 90 Days | Older |
|--------|---------|---------|---------|---------|-------|
| 0.00 | 0.00 | 0.00 | 437.34 | 0.00 | 0.00 |

[ Tidy List ]  [ Range ]

**4 Set the range**

| Save | Discard | Delete | Back | Next | Print List | | Close |

### Activity Date Range

**Transaction Range**

From: 12
To: 19

**Transaction Type**

Type to Display: All - All Transactions

Outstanding Transactions Only? ☐

**Date Range**

From: 01/06/2002
To: 30/07/2002

[ OK ]  [ Cancel ]

## Take note

The Delete button deletes the **record**, not a transaction. If you need to delete a transaction recorded in error, try the Corrections routine (see page 34).

76

# Aged analysis

**1** Open, or return to, the Customer window.

**2** Select the record(s).

**3** Click ![Aged].

**4** Set the report date and end date.

**5** Click Close.

The Aged Analysis can be run from the main Customer and Supplier windows. It shows the amounts owing, arranged into Ageing periods, as defined in the customer defaults.

> **3** Click Aged

> **Tip**
>
> **You can also use a Search (page 86) to track down old debts.**

> **2** Select the record(s)

**Customers**

| New | Record | Activity | Aged | Invoice | Credit | Charges | Phone | Labels | Letters | Statement | Reports |

**Customers** (All Records)

| A/C | Name | Balance | Crd Limit | Contact |
|-----|------|---------|-----------|---------|
| JONESG | Mr G. Jones | 58.16 | 500.00 | |
| JONESJ | Ms J. Jones | 0.00 | 500.00 | |
| PLUMPINS | Plumpton Institute | 0.00 | 2000.00 | Mr. Smith |
| PLUMPTC | Plumpton Town Council | 437.34 | 5000.00 | |
| REVGREEN | Rev Green | 75.81 | | |
| RIBBONS | Ribbons and Bows | 362.50 | | |
| SMITH01 | Mr & Mrs I Smith | 0.00 | | |
| WHITE | Mrs E. White | 425.00 | | |

Search | Swap | Clear | Delete | Print List

**Aged Balances Date Defaults**

Enter Range

Aged Balance Report Date    12/07/2002

Include Payments Up To    28/06/2002

OK | Cancel

> **4** Set the dates

**Aged Balances as of 12th July 2002**

Aged Balances | Graph

| A/C | YTD | Credit Limit | Balance | Future | Current | 30 Days | 60 Days | 90 Days |
|-----|-----|--------------|---------|--------|---------|---------|---------|---------|
| JONESG | 49.50 | 500.00 | 58.16 | | | 58.16 | | |
| JONESJ | 1542.00 | 500.00 | | | | | | |
| PLUMPINS | 0.00 | 2000.00 | | | | | | |
| PLUMPTC | 4946.00 | 5000.00 | 437.34 | | | | 437.34 | |
| REVGREEN | 65.00 | 500.00 | 75.81 | | 75.81 | | | |
| RIBBONS | 362.50 | 500.00 | 362.50 | | 362.50 | | | |
| SMITH01 | 0.00 | 500.00 | | | | | | |
| WHITE | 425.00 | 500.00 | 425.00 | | 425.00 | | | |

| Future | Current | 30 Days | 60 Days | 90 Days | Older | Balance | Debtors |
|--------|---------|---------|---------|---------|-------|---------|---------|
| 0.00 | 863.31 | 58.16 | 437.34 | 0.00 | 0.00 | 1358.81 | 1358.81 |

Detailed | Print List | Close

> **5** Click Close

# Batch Invoices

Invoices and credit notes will normally be dealt with through the Invoicing module, where they can be created, printed and the transactions posted to the ledgers. The Invoices and Credits routines in the Customer module are there to record the transactions when invoices or credit notes have been produced manually. In the Supplier module, they are the main way to record your transactions with suppliers.

## VAT-inclusive?

The system calculates VAT, whether prices are given Net or VAT-inclusive. Prices are always entered into the Net column.

♦ With Net prices, the VAT will appear automatically.

♦ With VAT-inclusive prices, click **Calculate Net** to split the total into the Net and VAT elements.

☐ Recording invoices

1 In the Customer window click [Invoicing].

2 Select the account from the A/C list.

3 Enter the date and other details.

4 Enter the Net amount.

5 If the price is VAT-inclusive, click Calc. Net.

6 Click Save.

7 Repeat as needed, then click Close.

2 Select the account

3 Enter details

4 Enter the amount

**Batch Customer Invoices**

Invoices

| A/C | Plumpton Institute | | | | | Tax Rate | 17.50 |
| N/C | General plumbing | | | | | Batch Total | 93.75 |

| A/C | Date | Ref | Ex.Ref | N/C | Dept | Details | Net | T/C | VAT |
|-----|------|-----|--------|-----|------|---------|-----|-----|-----|
| JONESJ | 01/07/2002 | 010702 | | 4000 | 0 | Blocked outfl | 29.79 | T1 | 5.21 |
| PLUMPINS | 03/07/2002 | 030702 | | 4000 | 0 | Punctured pip | 50.00 | T1 | 8.75 |
| | | | | | | | 79.79 | | 13.96 |

Save   Discard   Calc. Net                    Close

6 Click Save

5 Calculate Net and VAT?

7 Close

Tip

**Entries are normally a single line. If you want to record an invoice in detail, spread it over several lines, but using the same Refn code.**

# Credit notes

## Basic steps

1 Look up the Reference number of the invoice in the customer or supplier's Activity tab.

2 Click [Credit] in the Customer module.

3 Complete as for an invoice, but with the original Refn number.

These are handled in almost exactly the same way as invoices. The key point to note is that the reference number here must be that of the invoice against which the credit is being given.

1 Look up the reference number

In the details lines, this column holds the nominal code

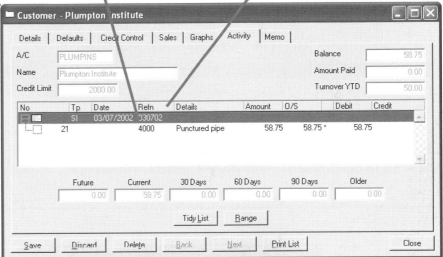

3 Use the same Ref number

# Printouts

Most of the printouts that you are likely to need can be obtained with just a few mouse clicks. There are ready-made labels, letters, statements and reports, some designed for output onto plain paper, others onto Sage stationery.

## Basic steps

1 Select the customer(s) to whom you want to send the printout.
2 Click a printout tool.
3 Select the layout.
4 To check it before printing, select Preview.
5 Click **Run**.

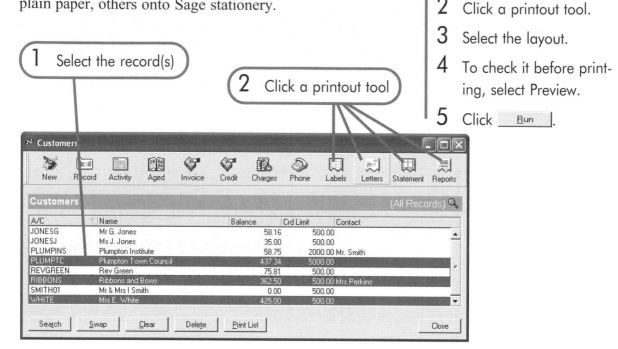

1 Select the record(s)

2 Click a printout tool

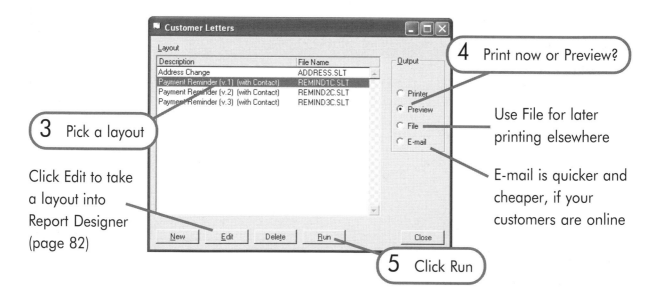

3 Pick a layout

Click Edit to take a layout into Report Designer (page 82)

4 Print now or Preview?

Use File for later printing elsewhere

E-mail is quicker and cheaper, if your customers are online

5 Click Run

The statements are all designed for use with
Sage stationery — if you print on plain
paper, none of the headings will appear.

G.A. Jones T/A PlumbCrazy
12 Coldmain Road
Plumpton
PL12 2QW

| To | PLUMPTC |
|---|---|

Plumpton Town Council
Town Hall
Main Street
Plumpton

| Date | 12/07/2002 |
|---|---|

STATEMENT

| Date | Ref. | Details | Invoice | Credit | Balance |
|---|---|---|---|---|---|
| 12/07/2002 | O/Bal | Goods/Services | 2,560.00 | | 2,560.00 |
| 14/06/2002 | 4 | Goods/Services | 437.34 | | 2,997.34 |
| 10/05/2002 | 3 | Goods/Services | 145.78 | | 3,143.12 |
| 10/05/2002 | 2 | Goods/Services | 291.56 | | 3,434.68 |
| 31/05/2002 | | Payment | | 4,500.00 | -1,065.32 |
| 28/06/2002 | | Payment | | 405.32 | -1,470.64 |

| Current | Period 1 | Period 2 | Period 3 | Older | | Amount Due |
|---|---|---|---|---|---|---|
| 0.00 | 0.00 | 437.34 | 0.00 | 0.00 | | 437.34 |

Tip

**If your printer's page set up does not match the printout's set up, you'll get an error message — use the Fix option, and let the system sort things out!**

# Report Designer

If none of the ready-made layouts meet your needs, you can edit them – you may want to add the Balance to your reminders – or create a new one from scratch. The same Report Designer window opens, whether you are working on a label, letter, statement or report.

You can get into the Report Designer in two ways.

All the module windows have toolbar buttons for letters, reports or whatever layouts are available in that module. The dialog boxes that open from these are mainly used to select layouts for printing, but they can also be edited from here (see page 80).

The Reports button on the main toolbar opens the Report Designer window, where you can access all of the many existing layouts or create a new one.

A layout document is made up of elements:

♦ **Variables** which draw data from your files. There are so many variables that a single list would be unwieldly, so they are grouped into data tables, each containing a related set.

♦ **Text**, written in separate boxes. Click **T** to start, then type the text – the box will expand as you type.

♦ **Lines** \ and boxes □, for marking off areas.

♦ **Expressions** (calculations on fields) started from ⅀ˣ⁼.

When you add a variable or an expression, the Active Complete dialog box opens. This can add a title and or a total for the variable, if required. In a report, where the data will typically be laid out in rows and columns, titles and totals are often wanted; on a letter, a variable is more likely to be placed as a single item by itself.

## Basic steps

1 Open the layout that you want to edit.

❑ To add a field

2 Select the data table, then the variable.

3 Click on the document to place the variable.

4 At the Active Complete dialog box, set the options to add a title and total, if required, then click OK.

*continued on page 84...*

**2** Select the table then the variable

**3** Click to place the variable

**4** Add a title and/or total?

You can set the size here, or when the variable is in place

Report Designer - [REMIND2C.SLT]

File Edit View Format Tools Window Help

100%

REPORT

REPORT
CRITERIA
COMPANY
SALES_LEDGER
AUDIT_HEADER
AUDIT_SPLIT
AUDIT_USAGE
TAX_CODE

Header Detail ▼  Times

ACCOUNT_REF
DATE_CREDIT_APPLIED
DATE_CREDIT_RECEIVED
OVERRIDE_TAX_CODE
LAST_PAYMENT_DATE
FIRST_INV_DATE
LAST_INV_DATE
BALANCE
TURNOVER_MTD
TURNOVER_YTD
PRIOR_YEAR

NAME
ADDRESS_1
ADDRESS_2
C_ADDRESS_3
C_ADDRESS_4
C_ADDRESS_5

DATE

NAME
C_ADDRESS_1
C_ADDRESS_2
C_ADDRESS_3
C_ADDRESS_4
C_ADDRESS_5

of our overdue account. The current balance is
appreciate your assistance in avoiding a suspension of deliveries,
d by return.

Page 1/1

**Active Complete**

Active Complete has detected that you are adding a new variable. You can use Active Complete to automatically add a title and total for your variable.

**Title**

Choose the position where you want the title to appear.

⦿ Do not add a title

○ Add a title in the section above where the variable was placed

○ Add a title to the left of the variable

Enter the text for the title

Balance

☑ Use variable width for title width

**Totals**

Active Complete can automatically add a total in either the next or all of the following footer sections.

⦿ Do not add a total

○ Only add a total in the next footer section

○ Add a total for all of the following footer sections

**Variable Size**

Output Length: 15    Width: 4.1275

☐ On completion display the Object Properties window
☐ Remember settings for this session

OK    Cancel

83

...continued

## Take note

To select a single object, click on it. To select several, either hold down [Shift] while you click on them, or drag the mouse across the objects. If an object is selected, handles will appear at both ends.

5 Click into the variable's box and drag to move it. Drag on a handle to resize it.

❑ To format text

6 Select the text box or variables.

7 Pick a new Style from the drop-down list.

Zoom level

7 Select a style

8 Click a button or pick from a drop-down list

**Report Designer - [REMIND2C.SLT]**

File   Edit   View   Format   Tools   Window   Help

100%

SALES_LEDGER        BALANCE

Header Detail ▾    Times New Roman ▾    10 ▾    **B**  *I*  <u>U</u>  ō    ≣ ≣ ≣

C_ADDRESS_2
C_ADDRESS_3
C_ADDRESS_4
C_ADDRESS_5

DATE

NAME
C_ADDRESS_1
C_ADDRESS_2
C_ADDRESS_3
C_ADDRESS_4
C_ADDRESS_5

Dear   CONTACT_NAME

We have written to your Payables Manager requesting payment of our overdue account. The current balance is BALANCE
Unfortunately the account remains unpaid and we would now appreciate your assistance in avoiding a suspension of deliveries, a step which we must reluctantly take if payment is not received by return.

Design   Preview

5 Move or resize to fit

To edit text, select the element then click into it to locate the editing cursor (|)

*Or*

**8** Pick a new font or size from the drop-down lists, or click a format button.

**9** The formatting can either be applied to the current Style or to the Selected objects – click a button as appropriate.

**10** Click Preview to see how the layout looks when variables are replaced with actual data.

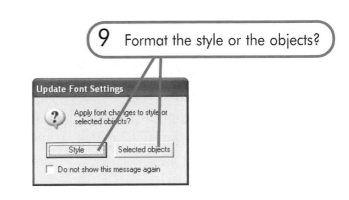

**9** Format the style or the objects?

**Update Font Settings**

? Apply font changes to style or selected objects?

[ Style ] [ Selected objects ]

☐ Do not show this message again

---

**Report Designer - [REMIND2C.SLT]**

File   Edit   View   Format   Tools   Window   Help

100%

G.A. Jones T/A PlumbCrazy
12 Coldmain Road
Plumpton
PL12 2QW

13 July 2002

Plumpton Institute
College Place
Plumpton
PL12 2PL

**Move through the records**

**10** Preview the document

We have written to your Payables Manager requesting payment of our overdue account. The current balance is 58.75. Unfortunately the account remains unpaid and we would now appreciate your assistance in avoiding a suspension of deliveries, a step which we must reluctantly take if payment is not received by return.

Design   **Preview**

Page 3/8

# Searching

If you only have a few customers and suppliers, and are reasonably familiar with the state of their accounts, it's no great bother to run through the list selecting them individually when you want to examine or process them. Once you get beyond a few, it's worth learning how to use the Search routine.

By specifying criteria, you can pick out those accounts where the values in a particular field match a given value. For example:

♦ the customers in a town,

♦ the suppliers whose invoices are due,

♦ trading partners where the annual turnover is over £10,000 or those below £500.

Conditions can be set on as many fields as necessary, to select very specific sets of records. Conditions can be joined by **And**, if both must apply, or **Or**, where records are selected if either or both conditions apply.

The example here is from the Customer module, but the Search routine is used in the same way in all modules.

## Basic steps

1 Click `Search`.

2 In the Join column, select *Where*.

3 Click into the Field column and select a field from the list.

4 Click into the Condition column and select one.

5 Type the Value.

6 If you want to set another condition, click into the Join box of the next line and select And or Or, then work through steps 3 to 5 again.

7 Click `Apply`, then `Close`.

| A/C | Name | Balance | Crd Limit | Contact |
|-----|------|---------|-----------|---------|
| JONESG | Mr G. Jones | 58.16 | 500.00 | |
| JONESJ | Ms J. Jones | 35.00 | 500.00 | |
| PLUMPINS | Plumpton Institute | 58.75 | 2000.00 | Mr. Smith |
| PLUMPTC | Plumpton Town Council | 437.34 | 5000.00 | |
| REVGREEN | Rev Green | 75.81 | 500.00 | |
| RIBBONS | Ribbons and Bows | 362.50 | 500.00 | Mrs Perkins |
| SMITH01 | Mr & Mrs I Smith | 0.00 | 500.00 | |
| WHITE | Mrs E. White | 425.00 | 500.00 | |

Customers — (All Records)

New  Record  Activity  Aged  Invoice  Credit  Charges  Phone  Labels  Letters  Statement  Reports

Search  Swap  Clear  Delete  Print List  Close

1 Click Search

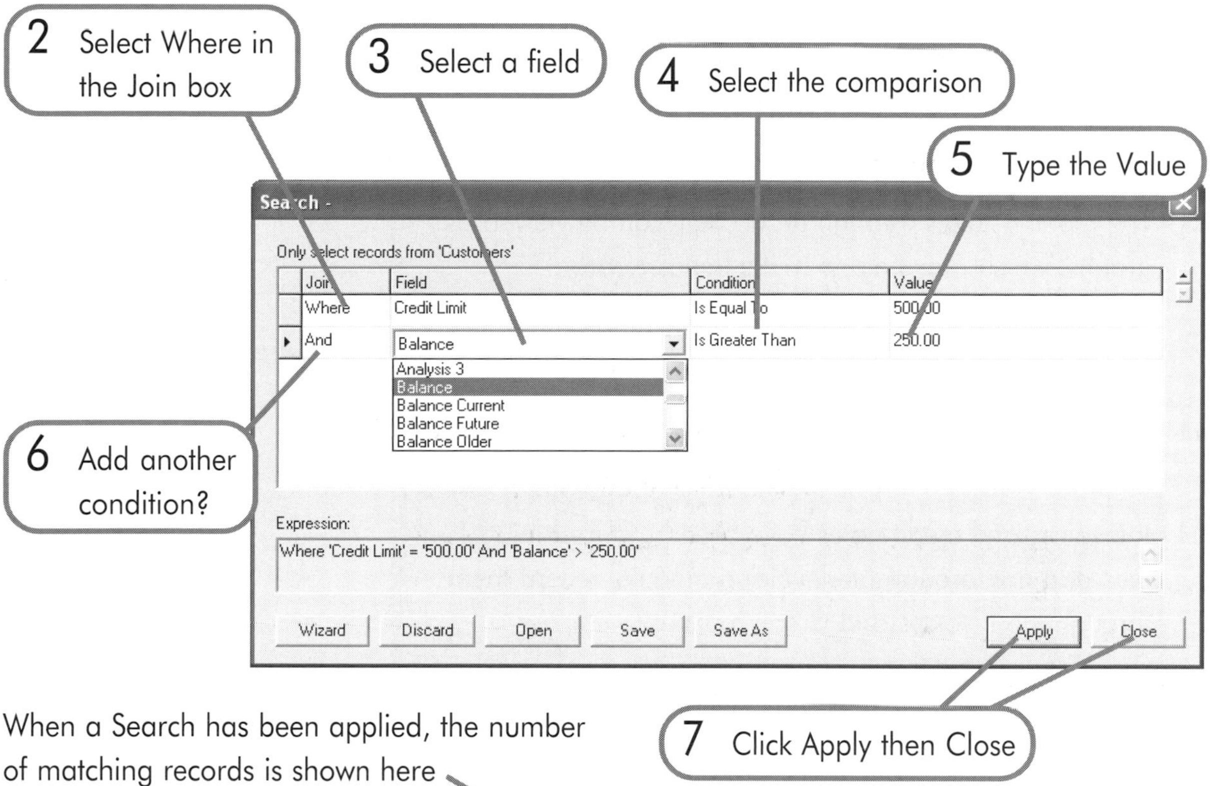

**2** Select Where in the Join box

**3** Select a field

**4** Select the comparison

**5** Type the Value

**6** Add another condition?

**7** Click Apply then Close

**Search -**

Only select records from 'Customers'

| | Join | Field | Condition | Value |
|---|---|---|---|---|
| | Where | Credit Limit | Is Equal To | 500.00 |
| ▶ | And | Balance | Is Greater Than | 250.00 |

Analysis 3
Balance
Balance Current
Balance Future
Balance Older

Expression:

Where 'Credit Limit' = '500.00' And 'Balance' > '250.00'

| Wizard | Discard | Open | Save | Save As | | Apply | Close |
|---|---|---|---|---|---|---|---|

When a Search has been applied, the number of matching records is shown here

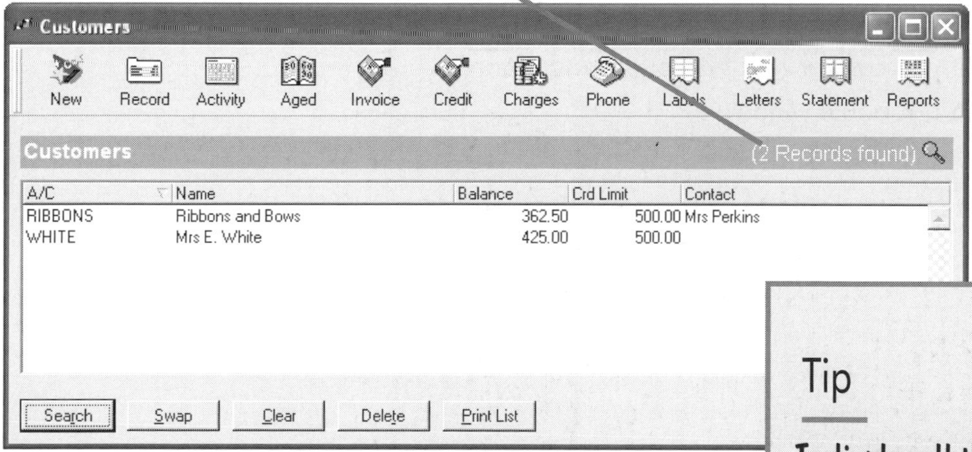

**Customers**

| New | Record | Activity | Aged | Invoice | Credit | Charges | Phone | Labels | Letters | Statement | Reports |

**Customers**                                          (2 Records found) 🔍

| A/C | Name | Balance | Crd Limit | Contact |
|---|---|---|---|---|
| RIBBONS | Ribbons and Bows | 362.50 | 500.00 | Mrs Perkins |
| WHITE | Mrs E. White | 425.00 | 500.00 | |

| Search | Swap | Clear | Delete | Print List |

## Tip

To display all the records again, reopen the **Search** dialog box and click the **Discard** button.

# Summary

❑ New Customer and Supplier accounts are easily set up using the Wizard.

❑ Records can be viewed and edited by selecting them from the list in the module window.

❑ The monthly totals through an account can be viewed as graphs, which may help to make trends clearer.

❑ The current transactions in an account can be examined through the Activity tab.

❑ The aged analysis facility will show what bills are overdue and by how long.

❑ If invoices and credit notes have been produced manually, and not through the Invoicing module, record them through the Invoices and Credit routines.

❑ Statements and letters can be easily printed whenever they are needed.

❑ Most printouts are designed for use with Sage pre-printed stationery. You can edit layouts in the Report Designer.

❑ A Search will let you control which accounts and records are displayed in a module window.

# 6 Invoicing

# The Invoicing module

The routines in the Invoicing module are used to create and print invoices and credit notes, and to post the transactions to the appropriate accounts in the Customer and Nominal ledgers.

Product and service invoices have different structures – which raises the question of what to do when the sales involve materials *and* labour. Here are two possible solutions:

♦ Set up labour as a 'Product', with the Sales price being the hourly rate. You may need several records for different types of skilled and unskilled labour. The job can then be processed through a Product invoice.

♦ Include materials in the details of a Service invoice. The catches with this are that you will have to calculate material costs, and that goods elements will not be posted automatically to the relevant Nominal accounts.

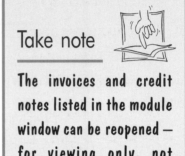

**Take note**

The invoices and credit notes listed in the module window can be reopened – for viewing only, not amendment. They are removed when the audit trail is cleared (page 116).

New invoice or credit note

Print invoices and notes

Update ledgers

Summary reports

| | | Invoicing | | | | | |
|---|---|---|---|---|---|---|---|
| New/Edit | Print | Update | Reports | | | | |

| No. | Type | Date | Name | Amount | Printed | Posted |
|---|---|---|---|---|---|---|
| 7 | Inv | 15/07/2002 | Mrs E. White | 744.42 | | |
| 6 | Scr | 24/05/2002 | Plumpton Town Council | 58.31 | | |
| 5 | Srv | 16/07/2002 | Plumpton Town Council | 1907.98 | Yes | |
| 4 | Srv | 14/06/2002 | Plumpton Town Council | 437.34 | Yes | |
| 3 | Srv | 10/05/2002 | Plumpton Town Council | 145.78 | Yes | |
| 2 | Srv | 10/05/2002 | Plumpton Town Council | 291.56 | Yes | |
| 1 | Inv | 09/07/2002 | Rev Green | 75.81 | Yes | |

Invoicing (All Records)

Search   Swap   Clear   Delete   Print List

**Take note**

Product and service invoices and credit notes are all started from the same New/Edit button.

## Basic steps

1 Click [New/Edit].

2 If *Invoice* is not the default Type, select it.

3 If *Product* is not the default Format, select it.

4 Set the Date.

5 Enter an Order No. if required.

6 Select the A/C code from the list.

7 Select the Product Code from the drop-down list. Its Description and Net price will be written in.

8 Enter the Quantity.

❑ Repeat steps 7 and 8 for each item, pressing [Tab] to open a new line.

9 Click [Save].

10 Repeat steps 2 to 8 for all invoices, and click [Close] at the end.

# Product invoices

The basic design of an invoice is the same whether it is for a product or a service. There are always:

◆ Invoice No – generated automatically.

◆ Date – also set for you, but can be changed if necessary.

◆ A/C Ref – selecting this pulls the name and address into the heading area on the top left.

◆ Order No. – if the customer has given one.

◆ VAT and the Totals – calculated by the system

In a Product invoice you also need to specify the items and the quantity of each.

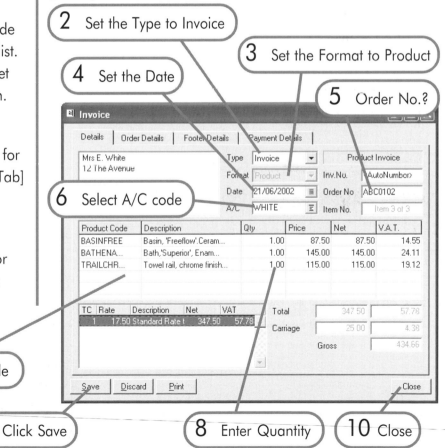

2 Set the Type to Invoice

3 Set the Format to Product

4 Set the Date

5 Order No.?

6 Select A/C code

7 Select Product Code

9 Click Save

8 Enter Quantity

10 Close

# Product descriptions and details

When you select a 'Special product', (code S1 or S2), the **Edit Item Line** dialog box will open to get the description, price and other details.

The same box can also be opened for any product if you need to adjust its details. Just click the ▣ icon on the right of the Description field.

## Basic steps

- ❑ Product details
- 1 Click ▣ by the Description field.
- 2 Edit the details and price as required.
- 3 To give a Discount, either give the percentage or the actual amount.
- 4 Click OK .

**2  Edit as required**

**Edit Item Line**  ☒

**Details**

| | | | |
|---|---|---|---|
| Product Code | S1 | Units | |
| Description | Fitting costs, per hour | | |
| Comment 1 | | | |
| Comment 2 | | | |

**Values**

| | | | | | |
|---|---|---|---|---|---|
| Quantity | 6.00 | Discount % | 0.0000 | Net | 150.00 |
| Unit Price | 25.00 | Discount | 0.0000 | VAT | 25.59 |

**3  Percentage or fixed discount?**

**Posting Details**

| | | | |
|---|---|---|---|
| Nominal Code | 4000 ▣ | Tax Code | T1 17.50 ▾ |
| Department | 0 | | ▾ |

**Job Details**

| | |
|---|---|
| Job Reference | |

Calc. Net          OK     Cancel

**4  Click OK**

## Tip

Make sure that no records are selected before you start to create an invoice or credit note.

# Basic steps

- ❏ Recording payments
- 1 Switch to the Payments Details panel.
- 2 Enter the amount.
- 3 Set any payment to the account or the invoice.
- ❏ Carriage and terms
- 4 Switch to the Footer Details panel.
- 5 Enter the Carriage.
- 6 Adjust the Terms as needed.
- ❏ Delivery
- 7 Go to the Order Details panel and enter the address and any notes.

# The Details panels

Many invoices can be completed simply using the top panel. The other panels allow you to add or adjust the details.

◆ Use the **Order Details** panel to record the delivery address and any notes.

◆ Use the **Footer Details** panel to add a carriage charge, or alter the default charge, or to adjust discounts and terms.

◆ If a payment has been received, this can be recorded on the **Payment Details** tab. The money can be allocated to that invoice, or as a general payment to the account.

## Product Invoice

| Details | Order Details | Footer Details | Payment Details |

**Payment Details**

Payment Ref: A123
Bank Account: 1200
Payment Amount: 436.17

**Payment Type**

○ Post as Payment on Account (SA)
● Allocate Payment to Invoice (SR)

1 Go to Payment

2 Enter the amount

3 Pay this invoice?

## Product Invoice

| Details | Order Details | Footer Details | Payment Details |

**Carriage**

Net: 25.00   Tax: T1 17.50
V.A.T.: 4.38   Gross: 29.38
N/C:   Dept.: 2 Sinkport branch
Consign. No:   Courier:

**Settlement Terms**

Days: 7   Amount: 8.70
Discount %: 2.50   Total: 427.47

**Global**

N/C:   Details:
Tax Code: T1 17.50   Dept.: 0

Save   Discard   Print   Close

4 Go to Footer Details

5 Enter the Carriage

6 Adjust the Terms?

# Service invoices

With a Service invoice, the nature of the work is written into the Details field. There can be any number of items, and the text for each can run over several lines, if required.

**1  Select Service**

**2  Type the Details**

**3  Enter the Amount**

**5  Click the Edit Item icon**

**8  Click Save**

**6  Edit the details**

**7  Click OK**

1  Begin as for a Product Invoice (page 91), but selecting *Service* as the Format.

2  Type the Details and press [Tab].

3  Enter the Amount.

4  To add an item, press [Tab] and repeat steps 2 and 3.

❑  Editing an item

5  Select the item and click ⊒.

6  Give a discount or edit the details as required.

7  Click   OK  .

8  Click   Save  .

## Tip

**To add a new line to the Description or Details of an item, press [Enter].**

**94**

## Basic steps

1 Check the details of the items in the invoice.

2 Begin as for an invoice, but selecting *Credit* as the Type.

3 Type the details and price of the credited item or service.

4 Click ☰ and edit the details/discount if required.

5 Enter any collection/ return information on the Order Details tab.

6 Click Save.

# Credit notes

Credit notes are the mirror image of invoices and produced in exactly the same way. Probably the most important thing with these is to make sure that they match the original invoice. Have prices changed since it was issued? Did you give a discount?

5 Enter return details?

2 Select Credit

**Product Credit**

Details | Order Details | Footer Details

| | | |
|---|---|---|
| Mrs E. White 12 The Avenue | Type | Credit | Product Credit |
| Redbridge | Format | Product | Crd.No. | <AutoNumber> |
| | Date | 16/07/2002 | Order No | |
| | A/C | WHITE | Item No. | Item 1 of 1 |

| Product Code | Description | Qty | Price | Net | V.A.T. |
|---|---|---|---|---|---|
| TRAILCHR... | e finish, 2 bar, floor fitting | 1.00 | 115.00 | 115.00 | 19.12 |

| TC | Rate | Description | Net | VAT | | Total | 115.00 | 19.12 |
|---|---|---|---|---|---|---|---|---|
| 1 | 17.50 | Standard Rate t | 115.00 | 9.12 | | Carriage | 0.00 | 0.00 |
| | | | | | | Gross | | 134.12 |

Save | Discard | Print | Close

6 Click Save

3 Enter the details

**Edit Item Line**

Details

| | | | |
|---|---|---|---|
| Product Code | TRAILCHROME2BAR | Units | |
| Description | Towel rail, chrome finish, 2 bar, floor fitting | | |
| Comment 1 | Supplied in error | | |
| Comment 2 | | | |

4 Edit or set discount?

Values

| | | | | | |
|---|---|---|---|---|---|
| Quantity | 1.00 | Discount % | 0.0000 | Net | 115.00 |
| Unit Price | 115.00 | Discount | 0.0000 | VAT | 13.12 |

Posting Details

| | | | | |
|---|---|---|---|---|
| Nominal Code | 4000 | Tax Code | T1 17.50 | |
| Department | 0 | | | |

Job Details

Job Reference

Calc. Net | OK | Cancel

## Take note

If you have allocated an early settlement discount to a customer, this will be reflected in the VAT calculation.

# Print and Update

## Printing

Whether you are printing one or many, the steps are the same. The difference is in how you start.

♦ With a single invoice or credit note, it is simplest to start from the **Print** button on the dialog box.

♦ If you are processing a set of transactions, it is more efficient to start printing from the Invoicing window.

❑ Printing

1 Click  in the dialog box.

*Or*

2 Select the records and click .

3 Pick a layout.

4 Select Preview to check the output on screen before printing, or Print to print immediately.

5 Click Run .

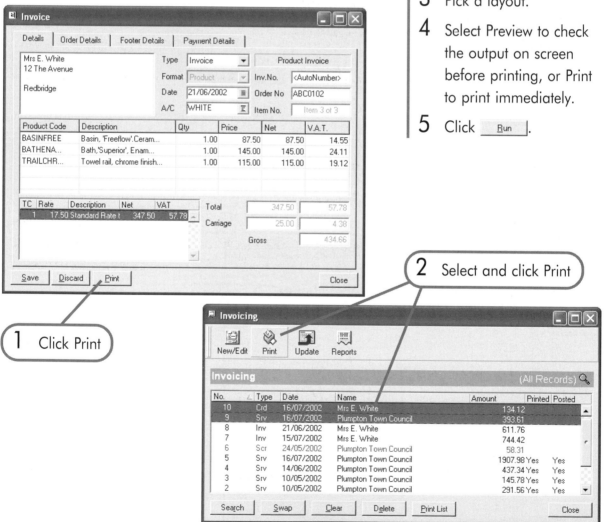

1 Click Print

2 Select and click Print

**96**

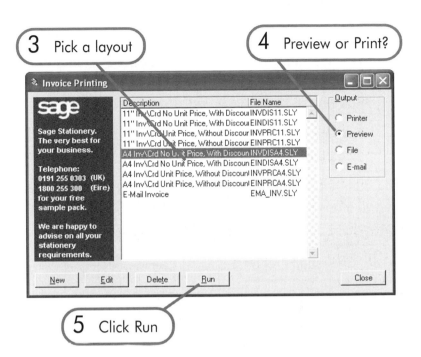
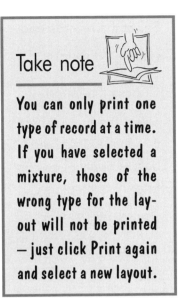

## Take note

You can only print one type of record at a time. If you have selected a mixture, those of the wrong type for the layout will not be printed — just click Print again and select a new layout.

❑ Updating

**6** Select the records.

**7** Click [Update].

**8** If a paper copy is needed, select Printer, otherwise select Preview.

**9** Click [OK].

## Updating ledgers

When you create and save an invoice or credit note, its information is stored in your files, but the effect of the transaction on other accounts is not recorded immediately. To 'post' the data to the relevant customers' and nominal accounts, you must use the **Update** button.

The system always shows the transactions it has performed. These can be output to paper or file, if required, or simply viewed on screen.

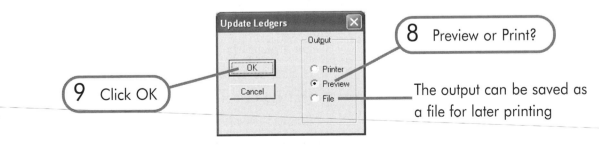

⑨ Click OK

⑧ Preview or Print?

The output can be saved as a file for later printing

# Reports

Three reports can be obtained from the Invoicing module.

♦ **Invoices not Printed** and **Invoices not Posted** give lists of those invoices and credit notes awaiting one or other process.

♦ **Invoice List (Summary)** is a printout of the information available in the module window.

The reports are simple lists, with a summary of each relevant record. You cannot change the layout, but you can set the font styles – you may well want to increase the font sizes!

## Basic steps

1 Select the records and click [Reports].

2 Choose the report.

3 Select Preview to check the output on screen before printing, or Print to print immediately.

4 Click [Run].

❑ Changing font styles

5 Click [Styles].

6 Select a style and click [Modify].

7 Set the Font, Style, Size and Effects – the Preview panel shows how it will look.

8 Click [OK].

9 Click [Close].

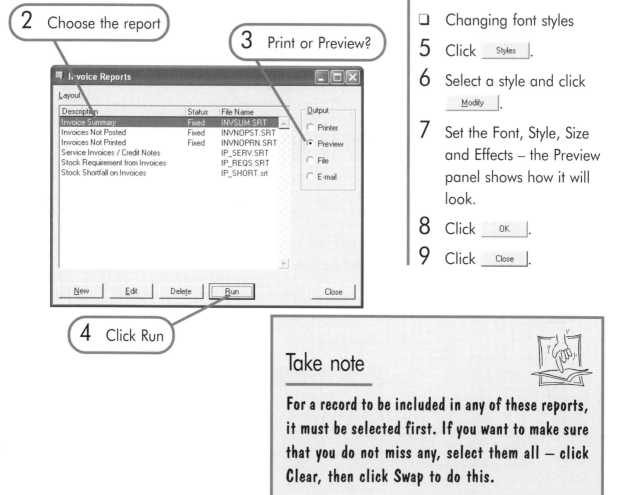

**2 Choose the report**

**3 Print or Preview?**

**4 Click Run**

## Take note

For a record to be included in any of these reports, it must be selected first. If you want to make sure that you do not miss any, select them all – click Clear, then click Swap to do this.

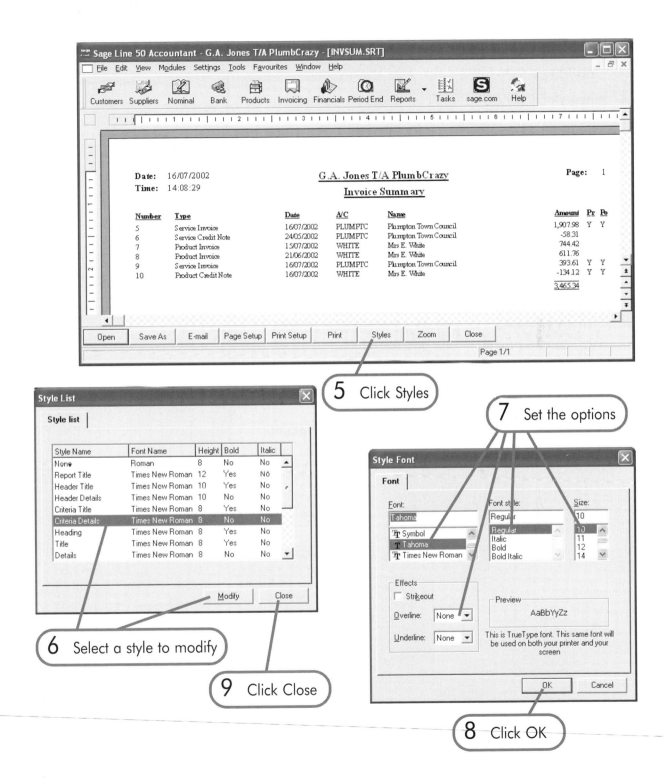

5 Click Styles

7 Set the options

6 Select a style to modify

9 Click Close

8 Click OK

# Summary

❑ Invoices and credit notes can be produced through the Invoicing module.

❑ When creating Product invoices, prices are taken from the relevant Product records. The details of each product can be adjusted, as necessary.

❑ With Service invoices, a job can be broken down into several items, each of which can be described over several lines.

❑ Credit notes are produced in the same way as invoices. The notes' reference numbers should match those of the original invoice.

❑ Each invoice can be printed as it is created, or a selected batch can be printed in one operation later.

❑ Transactions are not recorded in the relevant accounts until the Update ledgers routine is run.

❑ The reports from this module list invoices awaiting printing or updating, or all current invoices.

# 7 Bank accounts

# The Bank module

This module gives you a different view of, and more ways of working with, the Nominal accounts which are used for the payment and receipt of money.

In the Bank module, you can only select one record at a time – and for some operations, you don't need to select any.

## Basic steps

1 Select an account.

2 Click [Record].

3 View the information on the tabs.

4 Select another account from the A/C Ref list.

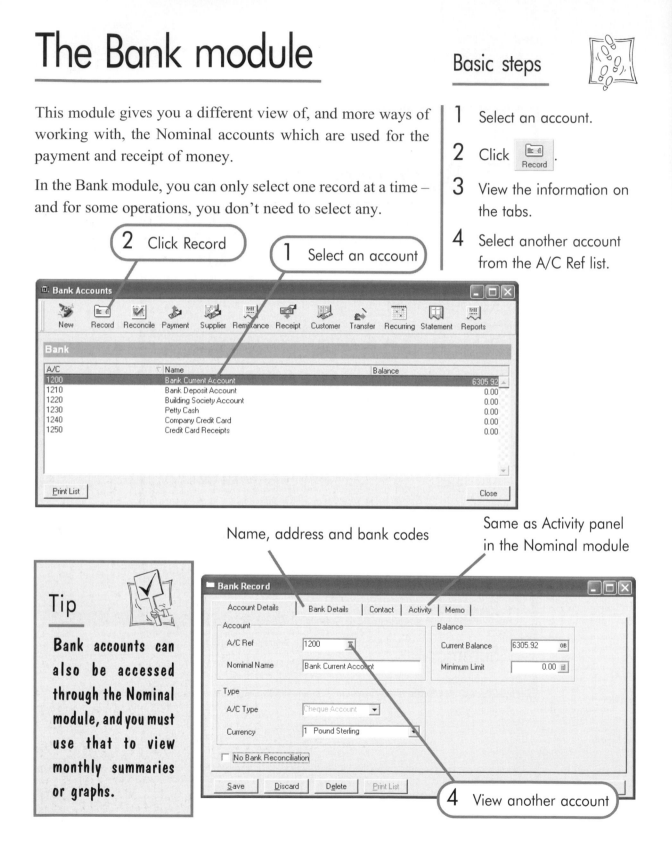

**2 Click Record**

**1 Select an account**

**Bank Accounts**

New  Record  Reconcile  Payment  Supplier  Remittance  Receipt  Customer  Transfer  Recurring  Statement  Reports

**Bank**

| A/C | Name | Balance |
|-----|------|---------|
| 1200 | Bank Current Account | 6305.92 |
| 1210 | Bank Deposit Account | 0.00 |
| 1220 | Building Society Account | 0.00 |
| 1230 | Petty Cash | 0.00 |
| 1240 | Company Credit Card | 0.00 |
| 1250 | Credit Card Receipts | 0.00 |

Print List                                            Close

Name, address and bank codes

Same as Activity panel in the Nominal module

## Tip

**Bank accounts can also be accessed through the Nominal module, and you must use that to view monthly summaries or graphs.**

**Bank Record**

Account Details | Bank Details | Contact | Activity | Memo

**Account**

A/C Ref          1200

Nominal Name     Bank Current Account

**Balance**

Current Balance  6305.92     OB

Minimum Limit    0.00

**Type**

A/C Type         Cheque Account

Currency         1  Pound Sterling

☐ No Bank Reconciliation

Save  |  Discard  |  Delete  |  Print List

**4 View another account**

102

# Basic steps

1 Select an account.

2 Click 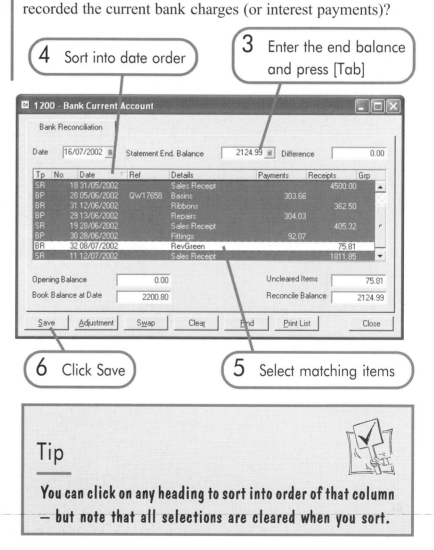 on the Bank Accounts toolbar.

3 Enter the End Balance from your bank statement and press [Tab] – the Difference will show the difference between the Opening and Statement End balances.

4 Click the Date heading to sort into date order.

5 Work through the list, clicking each item and marking its matching entry in the bank statement.

6 At the end, if the Difference is 0.00 and the Reconcile and Statement End balances match – click Save.

7 If the Difference is not 0.00, check the bank statement for charges or unmarked items.

# Reconciliation

Reconciliation is one of those chores that cannot be fully automated, but at least the Sage system makes it pretty straightforward. As you mark items that match entries in your bank statement, the system calculates and displays the difference between your recorded end balance and that of the bank statement. If they do not match after you have worked through the list, you can see how much it is adrift and will probably have a clear idea of the source of the problem. Have you, for instance, recorded the current bank charges (or interest payments)?

4 Sort into date order

3 Enter the end balance and press [Tab]

## 1200 - Bank Current Account

Bank Reconciliation

Date 16/07/2002  Statement End. Balance 2124.99  Difference 0.00

| Tp | No | Date | Ref | Details | Payments | Receipts | Grp |
|----|----|------|-----|---------|----------|----------|-----|
| SR | 18 | 31/05/2002 | | Sales Receipt | | 4500.00 | |
| BP | 28 | 05/06/2002 | QW17658 | Basins | 303.66 | | |
| BR | 31 | 12/06/2002 | | Ribbons | | 362.50 | |
| BP | 29 | 13/06/2002 | | Repairs | 304.03 | | |
| SR | 19 | 28/06/2002 | | Sales Receipt | | 405.32 | |
| BP | 30 | 28/06/2002 | | Fittings | 92.07 | | |
| BR | 32 | 08/07/2002 | | RevGreen | | 75.81 | |
| SR | 11 | 12/07/2002 | | Sales Receipt | | 1811.85 | |

Opening Balance 0.00   Uncleared Items 75.81
Book Balance at Date 2200.80   Reconcile Balance 2124.99

Save | Adjustment | Swap | Clear | End | Print List | Close

6 Click Save

5 Select matching items

## Tip

You can click on any heading to sort into order of that column – but note that all selections are cleared when you sort.

# Payments and Receipts

The Bank Payments and Bank Recipts routines are designed to handle cash transactions (credit transactions are recorded through the Customer and Supplier routines).

The example here is from the Bank Receipts panel, but exactly the same method is used to process payments.

## Basic steps

1  Select an account.

2  Click  or .

3  Select the Bank code.

4  Set the Date and give a Ref code if required.

5  Select the N/C number of the account for the goods or service.

6  Enter the Details of the sale or purchase.

7  Enter the amount into the Net box – if this is VAT-inclusive, click Calc. Net to split it into Net and VAT.

8  Repeat for other items.

9  Click Save .

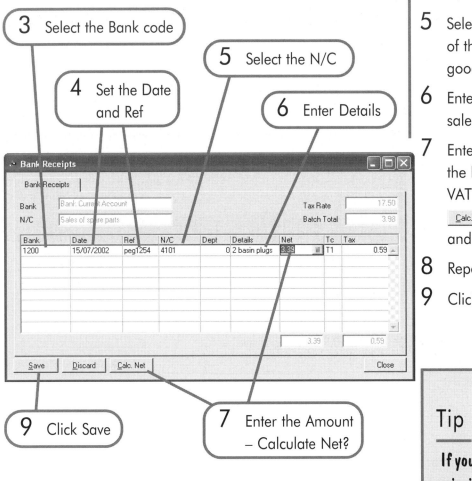

3  Select the Bank code

4  Set the Date and Ref

5  Select the N/C

6  Enter Details

9  Click Save

7  Enter the Amount – Calculate Net?

## Tip

**If you find that codes are missing from the N/C list, go to the Nominal module and clear the Search conditions.**

104

# Customer Receipts

## Basic steps

1   Select the bank account to take the money.

2   Click 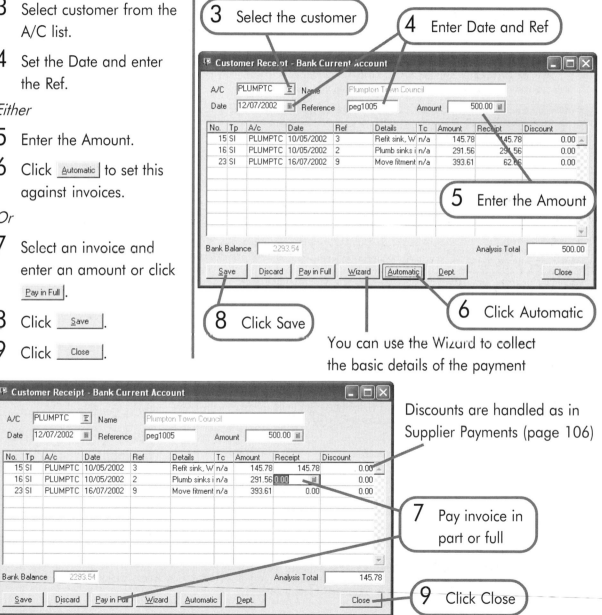.

    Customer

3   Select customer from the A/C list.

4   Set the Date and enter the Ref.

*Either*

5   Enter the Amount.

6   Click Automatic to set this against invoices.

*Or*

7   Select an invoice and enter an amount or click Pay in Full.

8   Click Save.

9   Click Close.

The Customer Receipts panel shows the outstanding invoices for the selected customer. Receipts can be allocated to specific invoices, or automatically set against invoices in references number (not *date*) order.

3   Select the customer

4   Enter Date and Ref

5   Enter the Amount

6   Click Automatic

8   Click Save

You can use the Wizard to collect the basic details of the payment

Discounts are handled as in Supplier Payments (page 106)

7   Pay invoice in part or full

9   Click Close

**105**

# Supplier Payments

The Sage systems won't write your cheques for you, but they will work out exactly how they should look! As you enter amounts against invoices, the system calculates the total and displays it in words and figures in the 'cheque' at the top.

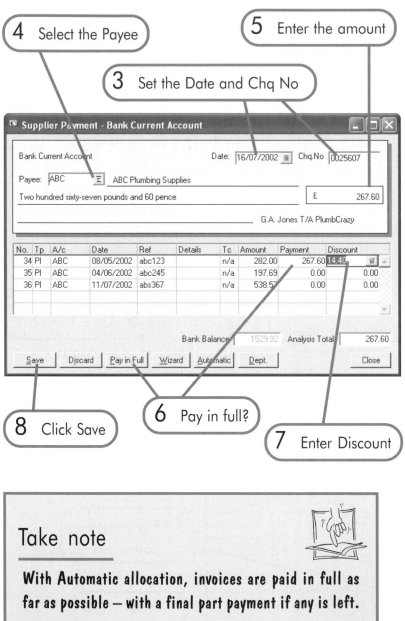

4 Select the Payee

5 Enter the amount

3 Set the Date and Chq No

**Supplier Payment - Bank Current Account**

Bank Current Account      Date: 16/07/2002   Chq.No 0025607

Payee: ABC    ABC Plumbing Supplies

Two hundred sixty-seven pounds and 60 pence      £    267.60

G.A. Jones T/A PlumbCrazy

| No. | Tp | A/c | Date | Ref | Details | Tc | Amount | Payment | Discount | |
|-----|----|-----|------|-----|---------|----|--------|---------|----------|--|
| 34 | PI | ABC | 08/05/2002 | abc123 | | n/a | 282.00 | 267.60 | 14.40 | |
| 35 | PI | ABC | 04/06/2002 | abc245 | | n/a | 197.69 | 0.00 | 0.00 | |
| 36 | PI | ABC | 11/07/2002 | abs367 | | n/a | 538.57 | 0.00 | 0.00 | |

Bank Balance 1529.92   Analysis Total 267.60

Save   Discard   Pay in Full   Wizard   Automatic   Dept.     Close

8 Click Save

6 Pay in full?

7 Enter Discount

## Take note

**With Automatic allocation, invoices are paid in full as far as possible – with a final part payment if any is left.**

1 Select the account from which the payment will be made.

2 Click [Supplier].

3 Set the Date and enter the Cheque No.

4 Select Payee from the drop-down list.

*Either*

5 Enter the amount on the 'cheque' and click Automatic to allocate this to invoices.

*Or*

6 Select an invoice and enter an amount or click Pay in Full.

❏ Discounts

7 Enter the full Payment, then the Discount – it will be deducted from the payment.

8 Click Save.

## Basic steps

1 Click .

2 Select the Account from which to transfer.

3 Select the Account to which the money will be transferred.

4 Set the Date.

5 Enter the Amount.

6 Edit the Details if 'Bank Transfer' does not say enough for you.

7 Click 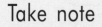.

Use this panel to record the movement of monies between Bank accounts. e.g. paying the credit card bill, or transferring cash between your current and deposit account at the bank.

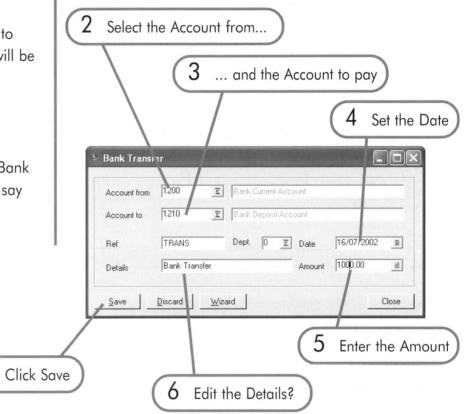

2 Select the Account from...

3 ... and the Account to pay

4 Set the Date

5 Enter the Amount

6 Edit the Details?

7 Click Save

## Take note

**Here, as elsewhere in the Bank routines, there is a Wizard, but it really isn't worth bothering with. It will just take you longer to enter the same information. Try it for yourself and see.**

# Recurring payments

Direct debits, standing orders and other regular payments can be set up as recurring entries and processed automatically.

Use this panel for adding or editing entries.

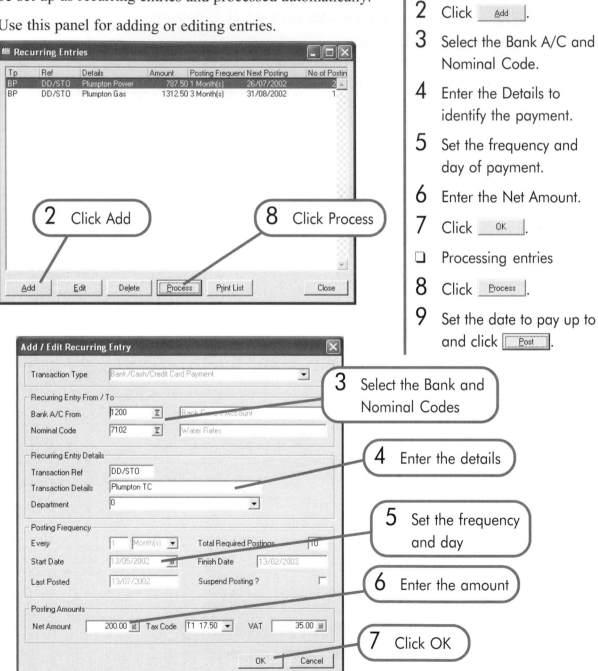

## Basic steps

1 Click [Recurring].

2 Click [Add].

3 Select the Bank A/C and Nominal Code.

4 Enter the Details to identify the payment.

5 Set the frequency and day of payment.

6 Enter the Net Amount.

7 Click [OK].

❑ Processing entries

8 Click [Process].

9 Set the date to pay up to and click [Post].

## Basic steps

1 Select the account.

2 Click 🔲 Statement .

3 Set the range by Date or Bank Ref.

4 Select the Output mode.

5 Click   OK  .

# Statements

The Statements button simply produces a list of the *reconciled* transactions, in numerical order, and the running balance for a selected account.

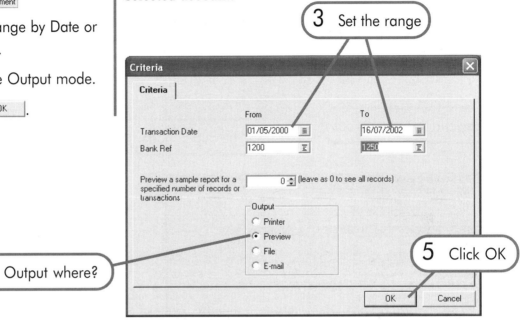

**3** Set the range

**Criteria**

| | From | To |
|---|---|---|
| Transaction Date | 01/05/2000 | 16/07/2002 |
| Bank Ref | 1200 | 1250 |

Preview a sample report for a specified number of records or transactions    0 (leave as 0 to see all records)

Output
- Printer
- Preview
- File
- E-mail

**4** Output where?

**5** Click OK

OK    Cancel

---

**BNKSTAT.SRT**

Date From:   01/01/1980
Date To:     16/07/2002

| No | Date | Ref | Details | Payments | Receipts | Balance |
|---|---|---|---|---|---|---|
| 11 | 12/07/2002 | | Sales Receipt | | 1,811.85 | 1,811.85 |
| 18 | 31/05/2002 | | Sales Receipt | | 4,500.00 | 6,311.85 |
| 19 | 28/06/2002 | | Sales Receipt | | 405.32 | 6,717.17 |
| 25 | 01/05/2002 | 10234 | Plastic pipes | 773.15 | | 5,944.02 |
| 26 | 07/05/2002 | QW14327 | Suites | 3,047.36 | | 2,896.66 |
| 27 | 24/05/2002 | 01256 | Copper pipes | 434.41 | | 2,462.25 |
| 28 | 05/06/2002 | QW17658 | Basins | 303.66 | | 2,158.59 |
| 29 | 13/06/2002 | | Repairs | 304.03 | | 1,854.56 |
| 30 | 28/06/2002 | | Fittings | 92.07 | | 1,762.49 |
| 31 | 12/06/2002 | | Ribbons | | 362.50 | 2,124.99 |
| 32 | 08/07/2002 | | RevGreen | | 75.81 | 2,200.80 |
| 33 | 16/07/2002 | | | | 3.99 | 2,204.79 |
| 37 | 15/07/2002 | peg1254 | 2 basin plugs | | 3.98 | 2,208.77 |
| 38 | 16/07/2002 | 0025607 | Purchase Payment | 267.60 | | 1,941.17 |
| 40 | 16/07/2002 | TRANS | Bank Transfer | 1,000.00 | | 941.17 |
| 42 | 26/05/2002 | DD/STO | Plumpton Power | 787.50 | | 153.67 |

Open   Save As   E-mail   Page Setup   Print Setup   Print   Styles   Zoom   Close

# Reports

The Sage system offers a range of summary and detailed reports, reflecting the accounts and transaction routines of the Bank module.

The layouts are all fixed, but you control the content by setting the range of dates and reference numbers, and by selecting the Nominal and Bank accounts to include.

## Basic steps

1 Select a Bank account.

2 Click  .

3 Select the Layout, either detailed or summary, choosing by the type of account or transaction.

4 Set the Ouput mode.

5 Click Run .

6 Set the range by Transaction Date …

7 … or by Transaction No..

8 Click OK .

**3 Select a suitable Layout**

**4 Set the ouput mode**

### Bank Reports

Layout

| Description | File Name |
|---|---|
| Bank Payments & Receipts by Bank Account | BN_PNRBB.SRT |
| Bank Report - Reconciled | BN_BANK2.SRT |
| Bank Report - Reconciled & Non Reconciled | BN_BANK1.SRT |
| Bank Report - Un-Reconciled | BN_BANK3.SRT |
| Day Books: Bank Payments (Detailed) | BNKBPD.SRT |
| Day Books: Bank Payments (Summary) | BNKBPS.SRT |
| Day Books: Bank Receipts (Detailed) | BNKBRD.SRT |
| Day Books: Bank Receipts (Summary) | BNKBRS.SRT |
| Day Books: Cash Payments (Detailed) | BNKCPD.SRT |
| Day Books: Cash Payments (Summary) | BNKCPS.SRT |
| Day Books: Cash Receipts (Detailed) | BNKCRD.SRT |
| Day Books: Cash Receipts (Summary) | BNKCRS.SRT |
| Day Books: Credit Card Payments (Detailed) | BNKVPD.SRT |
| Day Books: Credit Card Payments (Summary) | BNKVPS.SRT |
| Day Books: Credit Card Receipts (Detailed) | BNKVRD.SRT |

Output

- ○ Printer
- ● Preview
- ○ File
- ○ E-mail

Run     Close

**5 Click Run**

## Take note

You must select an account that matches the layout before opening the Reports panel. If you don't, and then try to run a report, it will grind away happily for a few moments before telling you that there is no information available.

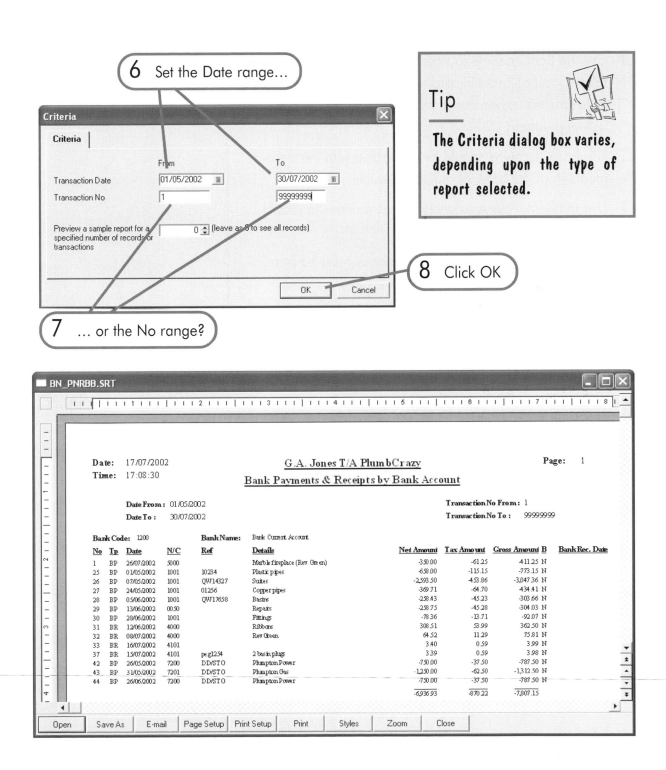

**6** Set the Date range...

**Criteria**

**Criteria**

| | From | To |
|---|---|---|
| Transaction Date | 01/05/2002 | 30/07/2002 |
| Transaction No | 1 | 99999999 |

Preview a sample report for a specified number of records or transactions **0** (leave as 0 to see all records)

OK    Cancel

**Tip**

The Criteria dialog box varies, depending upon the type of report selected.

**8** Click OK

**7** ... or the No range?

---

**BN_PNRBB.SRT**

| Date: | 17/07/2002 | | G.A. Jones T/A PlumbCrazy | | Page: | 1 |
| Time: | 17:08:30 | | Bank Payments & Receipts by Bank Account | | | |

| Date From : | 01/05/2002 | Transaction No From : | 1 |
| Date To : | 30/07/2002 | Transaction No To : | 99999999 |

**Bank Code:** 1200    **Bank Name:** Bank Current Account

| No | Tp | Date | N/C | Ref | Details | Net Amount | Tax Amount | Gross Amount | B | Bank Rec. Date |
|---|---|---|---|---|---|---|---|---|---|---|
| 1 | BP | 26/07/2002 | 5000 | | Marble fireplace (Rev Green) | -350.00 | -61.25 | -411.25 | N | |
| 25 | BP | 01/05/2002 | 1001 | 10234 | Plastic pipes | -658.00 | -115.15 | -773.15 | N | |
| 26 | BP | 07/05/2002 | 1001 | QW14327 | Suites | -2,593.50 | -453.86 | -3,047.36 | N | |
| 27 | BP | 24/05/2002 | 1001 | 01256 | Copper pipes | -369.71 | -64.70 | -434.41 | N | |
| 28 | BP | 05/06/2002 | 1001 | QW17658 | Basins | -258.43 | -45.23 | -303.66 | N | |
| 29 | BP | 13/06/2002 | 0050 | | Repairs | -258.75 | -45.28 | -304.03 | N | |
| 30 | BP | 28/06/2002 | 1001 | | Fittings | -78.36 | -13.71 | -92.07 | N | |
| 31 | BR | 12/06/2002 | 4000 | | Ribbons | 308.51 | 53.99 | 362.50 | N | |
| 32 | BR | 08/07/2002 | 4000 | | Rev Green | 64.52 | 11.29 | 75.81 | N | |
| 33 | BR | 16/07/2002 | 4101 | | | 3.40 | 0.59 | 3.99 | N | |
| 37 | BR | 15/07/2002 | 4101 | peg1254 | 2 basin plugs | 3.39 | 0.59 | 3.98 | N | |
| 42 | BP | 26/05/2002 | 7200 | DD/STO | Plumpton Power | -750.00 | -37.50 | -787.50 | N | |
| 43 | BP | 31/05/2002 | 7201 | DD/STO | Plumpton Gas | -1,250.00 | -62.50 | -1,312.50 | N | |
| 44 | BP | 26/06/2002 | 7200 | DD/STO | Plumpton Power | -750.00 | -37.50 | -787.50 | N | |
| | | | | | | -6,936.93 | -870.22 | -7,807.15 | | |

Open    Save As    E-mail    Page Setup    Print Setup    Print    Styles    Zoom    Close

# Summary

❑ Use the Bank module to view those Nominal accounts relating to bank, credit card and other cash accounts, and to record the movement of money to and from – and between – them.

❑ The Bank accounts should be reconciled with the statements from the bank at regular intervals.

❑ Use the Bank Payments and Receipts routines to record cash transactions.

❑ Use Customer Receipts to record money received from credit customers.

❑ Payments to your credit suppliers should be recorded through the Supplier Payments routine.

❑ When money is transferred between Bank accounts, it is recorded through the Transfers routine.

❑ Recurring payments can be set up and processed from this module.

❑ The Statements routine produces a simple list of transactions through Bank accounts.

❑ A wide range of Reports are available from the Bank module.

# 8 Financials

# The Audit trail

The Financials module contains tools for monitoring and analysing your accounts. A key part of this is the Audit Trail – the record of those transactions that have not yet been fully processed, and those processed but not yet cleared from the system.

The Audit Trail can be viewed, in summary form, in the Financials window. It can be printed out in the same form, or in briefer or more detailed forms through the **Audit** button. The printout routines also allow you to select the range of transactions by date, number, customer or supplier reference.

## Basic steps

1 Click .

2 Select the level of details.

3 Set the Output mode.

4 Click Run.

5 Set the limits on one or more criteria to define the range to display.

6 Click OK.

1 Click Audit

| No | Tp | Account | Nominal | Dep | Details | Date | Ref | Ex.Ref | Net | Tax | T/c | Paid |
|----|----|---------|---------|-----|---------|------|-----|--------|-----|-----|-----|------|
| 38 | PP | ABC | 1200 | 0 | Purchase Payment | 16/07/2002 | 0025607 | | 267.60 | 0.00 | T9 | Y |
| 39 | PD | ABC | 5009 | 0 | Purchase Discount | 16/07/2002 | 0025607 | | 14.40 | 0.00 | T9 | Y |
| 9 | SI | JONESG | 4000 | 0 | | 03/06/2002 | | | 49.50 | 8.66 | T1 | N |
| 10 | SI | JONESJ | 4000 | 0 | | 01/07/2002 | | | 1542.00 | 269.85 | T1 | Y |
| 11 | SR | JONESJ | 1200 | 0 | Sales Receipt | 12/07/2002 | | | 1811.85 | 0.00 | T9 | Y |
| 20 | SI | JONESJ | 4000 | 0 | Blocked outflow | 01/07/2002 | 010702 | | 29.79 | 5.21 | T1 | N |
| 21 | SI | PLUMPINS | 4000 | 0 | Punctured pipe | 03/07/2002 | 030702 | | 50.00 | 8.75 | T1 | Y |
| 49 | SI | PLUMPINS | 4000 | 0 | Annual maintenance, C block | 21/06/2002 | 11 | | 712.50 | 118.45 | T1 | Y |
| 50 | SI | PLUMPINS | 4000 | 0 | New radiators: 6 × 180 | 21/06/2002 | 11 | | 1026.00 | 170.57 | T1 | Y |
| 51 | SI | PLUMPINS | 4000 | 0 | Pipes and fittings | 21/06/2002 | 11 | | 150.10 | 24.95 | T1 | Y |
| 54 | SR | PLUMPINS | 1200 | 0 | Sales Receipt | 16/07/2002 | | | 2261.32 | 0.00 | T9 | Y |

**Financials** window toolbar: Audit, Trial, P and L, Balance, Budgets, Prior Yr, VAT, Reports

(All Records)

Search    Find    Close

Display only – items cannot be selected from here for closer inspection as they can in other modules

2 How much detail?

**Audit Trail Report**

Audit Trail Type
- ○ Brief
- ● Summary
- ○ Detailed
- ○ Deleted Transactions

Output
- ○ Printer
- ● Preview
- ○ File
- ○ E-mail

☑ Landscape Output    Run    Cancel

3 Output where?

4 Click Run

## Take note

You must get a full printout of the Audit Trail before running the clear routine (page 116).

114

# The Type codes

BP  Bank Payment

BR  Bank Receipt

JC  Journal Credit (e.g. bank transfer)

JD  Journal Debit

PC  Purchase Credit

PI  Purchase Invoice

PP  Purchase Payment

SA  Sale, payment on account

SC  Sale, Credit

SI  Sale, Invoice

SR  Sale Receipt

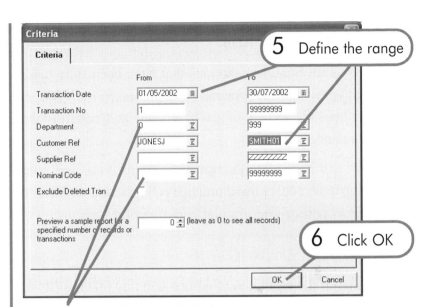

**5** Define the range

**6** Click OK

Department and Nominal Code only available for Summary lists

Long details can overrun!

VAT and Bank
Reconciled  Not reconciled

**Criteria**

| | From | To |
|---|---|---|
| Transaction Date | 01/05/2002 | 30/07/2002 |
| Transaction No | 1 | 99999999 |
| Department | 0 | 999 |
| Customer Ref | JONESJ | SMITH01 |
| Supplier Ref | | ZZZZZZZ |
| Nominal Code | | 99999999 |
| Exclude Deleted Tran | | |

Preview a sample report for a specified number of records or transactions    0    (leave as 0 to see all records)

OK    Cancel

---

■ AUDITSL.SRT

Date: 18/07/2002
Time: 11:13:59

G.A. Jones T/A PlumbCrazy
Audit Trail (Summary)

Page: 1

Date From: 01/05/2002
Date To: 30/07/2002

Customer From: JONESJ
Customer To: SMITH01

Transaction From: 1
Transaction To: 99999999

Supplier From:
Supplier To: ZZZZZZZ

Dept From: 0
Dept To: 999

N/C From:
N/C To: 99999999

Exclude Deleted Tran: No

| No | Type | Date | A/C | N/C | Dept | Refn | Details | Net | Tax | T/C | Pd | Paid | V | B |
|---|---|---|---|---|---|---|---|---|---|---|---|---|---|---|
| 7 | SI | 12.07.2002 | PLUMPTC | 9998 | 0 | O/Bal | Opening Balance | 2,560.00 | 0.00 | T9 | Y | 2,560.00 | - | - |
| 8 | SI | 12.07.2002 | RIBBONS | 9998 | 0 | O/Bal | Opening Balance | 362.50 | 0.00 | T9 | N | 0.00 | - | - |
| 10 | SI | 01.07.2002 | JONESJ | 4000 | 0 | | | 1,542.00 | 269.85 | T1 | Y | 1,811.85 | N | - |
| 11 | SR | 12.07.2002 | JONESJ | 1200 | 0 | | Sales Receipt | 1,811.85 | 0.00 | T9 | Y | 1,811.85 | - | R |
| 12 | SI | 16.07.2002 | PLUMPTC | 4000 | 0 | 5 | Chairpersons private washroom, installa | 650.00 | 108.06 | T1 | Y | 758.06 | N | - |
| 13 | SI | 16.07.2002 | PLUMPTC | 4000 | 0 | 5 | 3-piece suite in ivory, gold taps | 986.00 | 163.92 | T1 | Y | 1,149.92 | N | - |
| 14 | SI | 14.06.2002 | PLUMPTC | 4000 | 0 | 4 | Annual Boiler Service | 375.00 | 62.34 | T1 | Y | 437.34 | N | - |
| 15 | SI | 10.05.2002 | PLUMPTC | 4000 | 0 | 3 | Refit sink, WEst building | 125.00 | 20.78 | T1 | N | 0.00 | N | - |
| 16 | SI | 10.05.2002 | PLUMPTC | 4000 | 0 | 2 | Plumb sinks in new washroom, Westbuild | 250.00 | 41.56 | T1 | N | 0.00 | N | - |
| 17 | SI | 09.07.2002 | REVGREEN | 4000 | 0 | 1 | Adjust leaking valves (x3) | 65.00 | 10.81 | T1 | N | 0.00 | N | - |
| 18 | SI | 31.05.2002 | PLUMPTC | 1200 | 0 | | Sales Receipt | 4,500.00 | 0.00 | T9 | Y | 4,500.00 | - | R |
| 19 | SR | 28.06.2002 | PLUMPTC | 1200 | 0 | | Sales Receipt | 405.32 | 0.00 | T9 | Y | 405.32 | - | R |
| 20 | SI | 01.07.2002 | JONESJ | 4000 | 0 | 010702 | Blocked outflow | 29.79 | 5.21 | T1 | Y | 0.00 | N | - |
| 21 | SI | 03.07.2002 | PLUMPINS | 4000 | 0 | 030702 | Punctured pipe | 50.00 | 8.75 | T1 | Y | 58.75 | N | - |
| 23 | SI | 16.07.2002 | PLUMPINS | 4000 | 0 | 9 | Move fitments and replumb mayor's washroom | 300.60 | 49.88 | T1 | N | 0.00 | N | - |
| 24 | SI | 16.07.2002 | PLUMPTC | 4000 | 1 | 9 | Materials: 10m pipe 3.75 | 37.50 | 6.23 | T1 | N | 0.00 | N | - |
| 48 | SI | 01.07.2002 | SMITH01 | 4000 | 0 | 12 | Central heating installation | 2,540.00 | 422.28 | T1 | N | 1,500.00 | N | - |
| 49 | SI | 21.06.2002 | PLUMPINS | 4000 | 0 | 11 | Annual maintenance, C block | 712.50 | 118.45 | T1 | Y | 830.95 | N | - |
| 50 | SI | 21.06.2002 | PLUMPINS | 4000 | 0 | 11 | New radiators: 6 X 180 | 1,026.00 | 170.57 | T1 | Y | 1,196.57 | N | - |
| 51 | SI | 21.06.2002 | PLUMPINS | 4000 | 0 | 11 | Pipes and fittings | 150.10 | 24.95 | T1 | Y | 175.05 | N | - |
| 53 | SC | 24.05.2002 | PLUMPTC | 4000 | 0 | 6 | Correction of overcharge in error | 50.00 | 8.31 | T1 | N | 0.00 | N | - |
| 54 | SR | 16.07.2002 | PLUMPINS | 1200 | 0 | | Sales Receipt | 2,061.32 | 0.00 | T9 | Y | 2,061.32 | - | R |

Open   Save As   E-mail   Page Setup   Print Setup   Print   Styles   Zoom   Close

# End of period routines

## Basic steps

## Clearing the Audit Trail

Clearance removes all transactions that have been fully paid, reconciled with the bank statement and processed for VAT. It also calculates the effect of each account and rewrites the opening balances.

How long you keep a transaction 'live' is for you, and your accountant, to decide. Normal practice is for the Aaudit Trail to be cleared as part of your regular end of period routines.

## Month end

The purpose of the month end routines is to tidy up the system, so that you don't have to wade through old data, but to do this without losing any essential information.

◆ You must **make backups** – Sage recommends that you take one backup before running the VAT analysis and clearing the Audit Trail, and another afterwards.

◆ **Print** aged analysis, day books, statements and activity reports on all ledgers, plus the Audit Trail and Trial Balance.

1 Backup your files!

2 Print summary reports for all accounts.

3 Open the Tools menu, point to Period End and select Month End...

4 Tick Clear Turnover Figures and click OK .

5 You will be prompted to confirm the job – click Yes .

6 Open the Tools menu, Period End and select Clear Audit Trail...

7 Check the Date and click OK .

8 Click Yes .

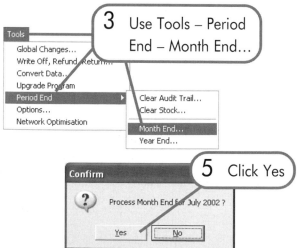

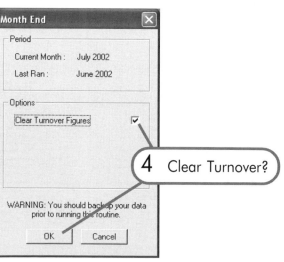

116

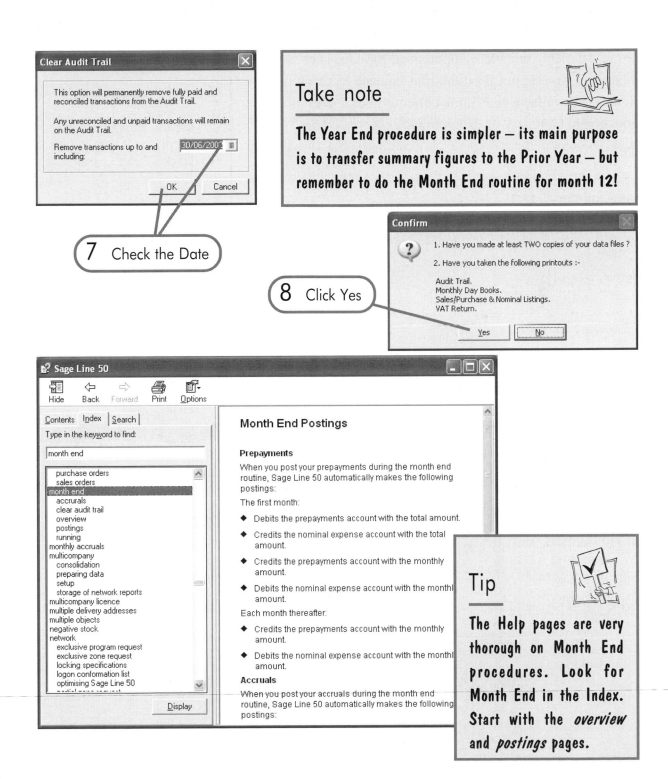

**Clear Audit Trail**

This option will permanently remove fully paid and reconciled transactions from the Audit Trail.

Any unreconciled and unpaid transactions will remain on the Audit Trail.

Remove transactions up to and including: 30/06/2003

OK    Cancel

**7** Check the Date

## Take note

The Year End procedure is simpler – its main purpose is to transfer summary figures to the Prior Year – but remember to do the Month End routine for month 12!

**Confirm**

1. Have you made at least TWO copies of your data files ?

2. Have you taken the following printouts :-

Audit Trail.
Monthly Day Books.
Sales/Purchase & Nominal Listings.
VAT Return.

Yes    No

**8** Click Yes

**Sage Line 50**

Hide  Back  Forward  Print  Options

Contents | Index | Search

Type in the keyword to find:

month end

purchase orders
sales orders
month end
  accruals
  clear audit trail
  overview
  postings
  running
monthly accruals
multicompany
  consolidation
  preparing data
  setup
  storage of network reports
multicompany licence
multiple delivery addresses
multiple objects
negative stock
network
  exclusive program request
  exclusive zone request
  locking specifications
  logon conformation list
  optimising Sage Line 50

Display

### Month End Postings

**Prepayments**

When you post your prepayments during the month end routine, Sage Line 50 automatically makes the following postings:

The first month:

◆ Debits the prepayments account with the total amount.

◆ Credits the nominal expense account with the total amount.

◆ Credits the prepayments account with the monthly amount.

◆ Debits the nominal expense account with the monthly amount.

Each month thereafter:

◆ Credits the prepayments account with the monthly amount.

◆ Debits the nominal expense account with the monthly amount.

**Accruals**

When you post your accruals during the month end routine, Sage Line 50 automatically makes the following postings:

## Tip

The Help pages are very thorough on Month End procedures. Look for Month End in the Index. Start with the *overview* and *postings* pages.

# The Trial Balance

In an efficient, reliable computerised system, such as Sage Accounts, you do not need the trial balance to check that the double-entries have been done correctly, but it does provide a convenient summary of the Nominal ledger accounts.

The Trial Balance is based on the data from the start of the year up to a chosen month – and, apart from the output mode, that is your only option.

## Basic steps

1 Click [Trial].

2 Select the end month.

3 Set the Output mode.

4 Click OK.

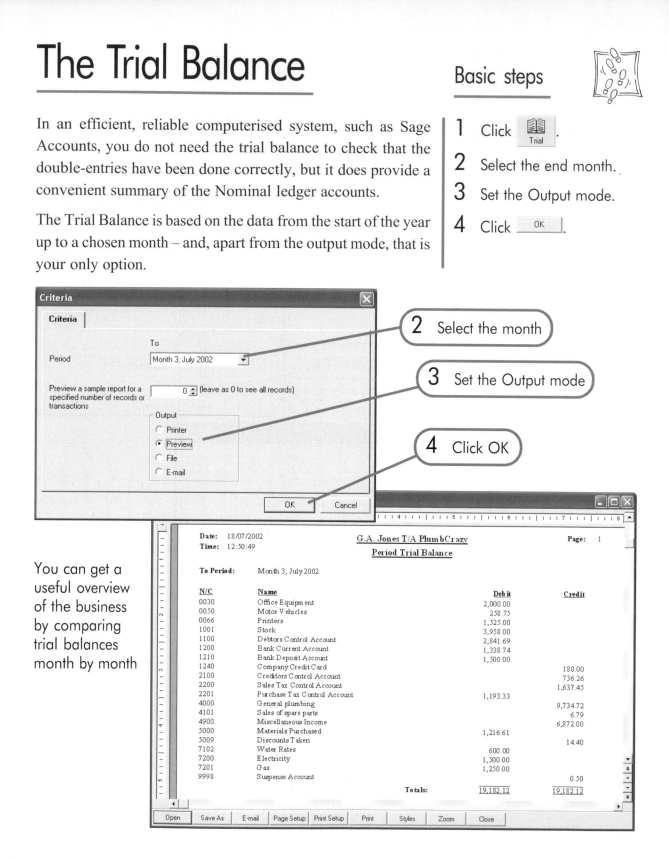

**2** Select the month

**3** Set the Output mode

**4** Click OK

You can get a useful overview of the business by comparing trial balances month by month

**Criteria**

Period — To — Month 3, July 2002

Preview a sample report for a specified number of records or transactions: 0 (leave as 0 to see all records)

Output:
- Printer
- Preview
- File
- E-mail

OK   Cancel

Date: 18/07/2002
Time: 12:50:49
G.A. Jones T/A PlumbCrazy
Period Trial Balance
Page: 1

To Period: Month 3, July 2002

| N/C | Name | Debit | Credit |
|---|---|---|---|
| 0030 | Office Equipment | 2,000.00 | |
| 0050 | Motor Vehicles | 258.75 | |
| 0066 | Printers | 1,525.00 | |
| 1001 | Stock | 3,958.00 | |
| 1100 | Debtors Control Account | 2,841.69 | |
| 1200 | Bank Current Account | 1,338.74 | |
| 1210 | Bank Deposit Account | 1,500.00 | |
| 1240 | Company Credit Card | | 180.00 |
| 2100 | Creditors Control Account | | 736.26 |
| 2200 | Sales Tax Control Account | | 1,637.45 |
| 2201 | Purchase Tax Control Account | 1,193.33 | |
| 4000 | General plumbing | | 9,734.72 |
| 4101 | Sales of spare parts | | 6.79 |
| 4900 | Miscellaneous Income | | 6,872.00 |
| 5000 | Materials Purchased | 1,216.61 | |
| 5009 | Discounts Taken | | 14.40 |
| 7102 | Water Rates | 600.00 | |
| 7200 | Electricity | 1,500.00 | |
| 7201 | Gas | 1,250.00 | |
| 9998 | Suspense Account | | 0.50 |
| | Totals: | 19,182.12 | 19,182.12 |

Open | Save As | E-mail | Page Setup | Print Setup | Print | Styles | Zoom | Close

## Basic steps

1 Click [P and L].

2 Select the start and end months.

3 Select a Chart of Accounts if desired.

4 Set the Output mode.

5 Click [OK].

# Profit and Loss account

With the Profit and Loss account, you define the period, allowing you to examine a month or quarter at any point of the year. You can also select the Chart of Accounts, if you have set up one or more of your own.

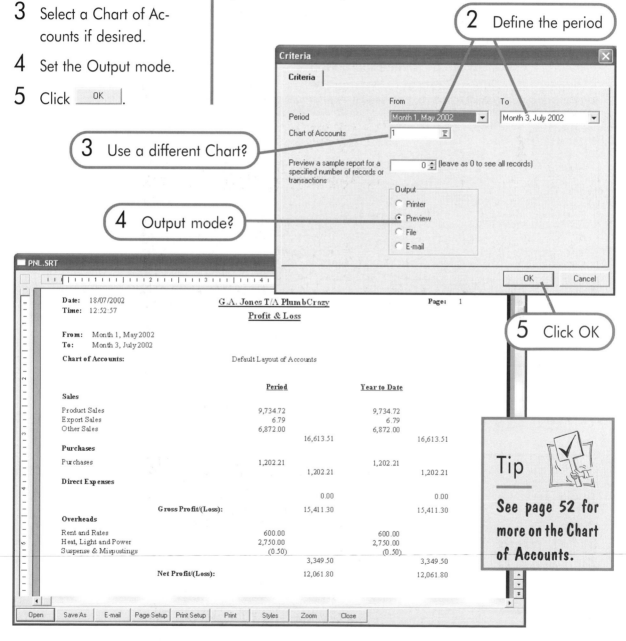

( 2 Define the period )

( 3 Use a different Chart? )

( 4 Output mode? )

( 5 Click OK )

**Criteria**

Criteria

| | From | To |
|---|---|---|
| Period | Month 1, May 2002 | Month 3, July 2002 |
| Chart of Accounts | 1 | |

Preview a sample report for a specified number of records or transactions    0  (leave as 0 to see all records)

Output
- Printer
- Preview
- File
- E-mail

[OK] [Cancel]

**PNL.SRT**

Date: 18/07/2002
Time: 12:52:57

G.A. Jones T/A PlumbCrazy    Page: 1
Profit & Loss

From: Month 1, May 2002
To: Month 3, July 2002

Chart of Accounts:    Default Layout of Accounts

| | Period | Year to Date |
|---|---|---|
| **Sales** | | |
| Product Sales | 9,734.72 | 9,734.72 |
| Export Sales | 6.79 | 6.79 |
| Other Sales | 6,872.00 | 6,872.00 |
| | 16,613.51 | 16,613.51 |
| **Purchases** | | |
| Purchases | 1,202.21 | 1,202.21 |
| | 1,202.21 | 1,202.21 |
| **Direct Expenses** | | |
| | 0.00 | 0.00 |
| Gross Profit/(Loss): | 15,411.30 | 15,411.30 |
| **Overheads** | | |
| Rent and Rates | 600.00 | 600.00 |
| Heat, Light and Power | 2,750.00 | 2,750.00 |
| Suspense & Mispostings | (0.50) | (0.50) |
| | 3,349.50 | 3,349.50 |
| Net Profit/(Loss): | 12,061.80 | 12,061.80 |

[Open] [Save As] [E-mail] [Page Setup] [Print Setup] [Print] [Styles] [Zoom] [Close]

Tip

See page 52 for more on the Chart of Accounts.

# The Balance Sheet

The Balance Sheet – and the Budget and Prior Year outputs – have the same options as the Profit and Loss account.

*Output to File* is worth considering on all of these. If the data is saved as either text or CSV (Comma Separated Values), it can be imported into a spreadsheet for further analysis.

Basic steps

1 Click  Budgets .

2 Select the start and end months.

3 Select a Chart of Accounts.

4 Set the Output mode.

5 Click  OK .

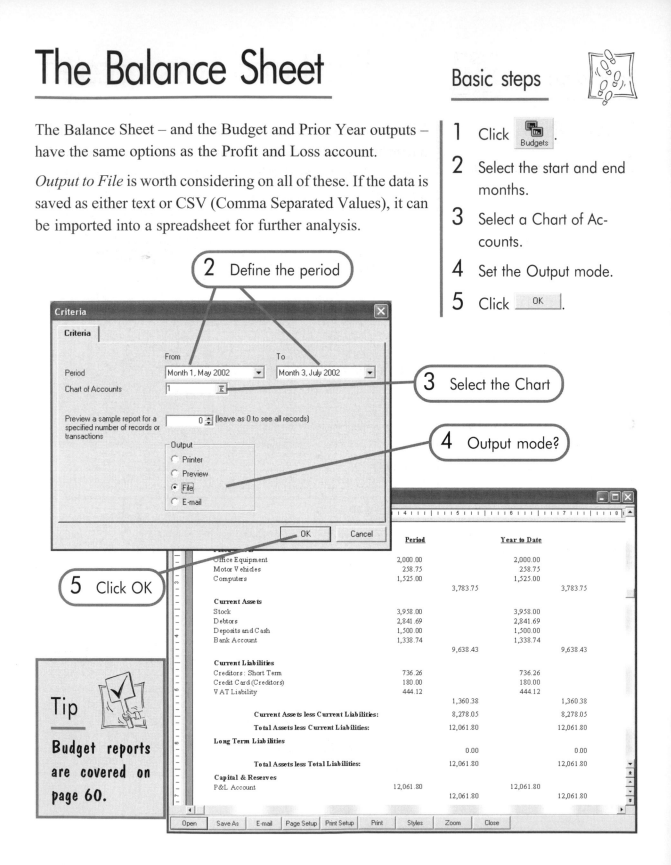

2 Define the period

3 Select the Chart

4 Output mode?

5 Click OK

**Tip**

Budget reports are covered on page 60.

**Criteria**

| | From | To |
|---|---|---|
| Period | Month 1, May 2002 | Month 3, July 2002 |
| Chart of Accounts | 1 | |

Preview a sample report for a specified number of records or transactions: 0 (leave as 0 to see all records)

Output
- Printer
- Preview
- File
- E-mail

OK    Cancel

| | Period | Year to Date |
|---|---|---|
| Office Equipment | 2,000.00 | 2,000.00 |
| Motor Vehicles | 258.75 | 258.75 |
| Computers | 1,525.00 | 1,525.00 |
| | 3,783.75 | 3,783.75 |
| **Current Assets** | | |
| Stock | 3,958.00 | 3,958.00 |
| Debtors | 2,841.69 | 2,841.69 |
| Deposits and Cash | 1,500.00 | 1,500.00 |
| Bank Account | 1,338.74 | 1,338.74 |
| | 9,638.43 | 9,638.43 |
| **Current Liabilities** | | |
| Creditors : Short Term | 736.26 | 736.26 |
| Credit Card (Creditors) | 180.00 | 180.00 |
| VAT Liability | 444.12 | 444.12 |
| | 1,360.38 | 1,360.38 |
| Current Assets less Current Liabilities: | 8,278.05 | 8,278.05 |
| Total Assets less Current Liabilities: | 12,061.80 | 12,061.80 |
| **Long Term Liabilities** | | |
| | 0.00 | 0.00 |
| Total Assets less Total Liabilities: | 12,061.80 | 12,061.80 |
| **Capital & Reserves** | | |
| P&L Account | 12,061.80 | 12,061.80 |
| | 12,061.80 | 12,061.80 |

Open  Save As  E-mail  Page Setup  Print Setup  Print  Styles  Zoom  Close

# Basic steps

1 Click ▓▓▓ .
     VAT

2 Select the start and end.

3 Click Calculate . You will be reminded to check all your figures before transferring them to your VAT return.

4 Click Print .

5 Select the Return Type and Output and click OK .

6 To mark transactions as processed, click Reconcile .

7 Click Close .

I like the way VAT is handled. In the same way that the payments screen mimics a cheque, so this screen follows the design of the standard VAT form. It makes transferring figures a breeze!

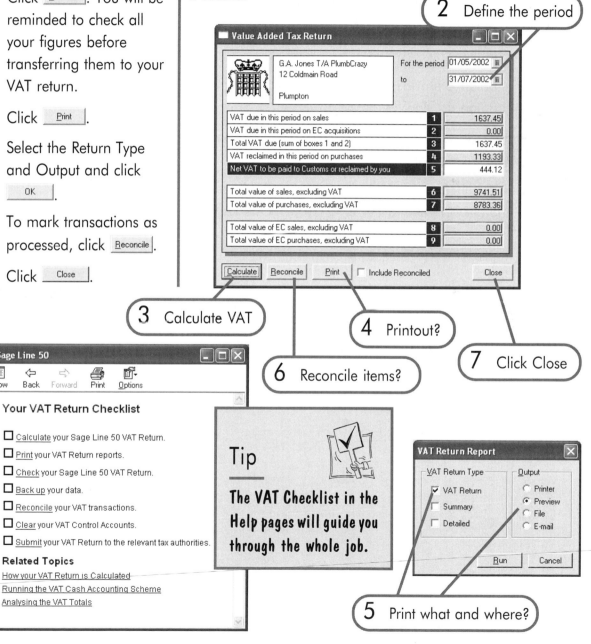

**2**   Define the period

**Value Added Tax Return**

G.A. Jones T/A PlumbCrazy
12 Coldmain Road
Plumpton

For the period 01/05/2002
to 31/07/2002

| | | |
|---|---|---|
| VAT due in this period on sales | 1 | 1637.45 |
| VAT due in this period on EC acquisitions | 2 | 0.00 |
| Total VAT due (sum of boxes 1 and 2) | 3 | 1637.45 |
| VAT reclaimed in this period on purchases | 4 | 1193.33 |
| Net VAT to be paid to Customs or reclaimed by you | 5 | 444.12 |
| Total value of sales, excluding VAT | 6 | 9741.51 |
| Total value of purchases, excluding VAT | 7 | 8783.36 |
| Total value of EC sales, excluding VAT | 8 | 0.00 |
| Total value of EC purchases, excluding VAT | 9 | 0.00 |

Calculate   Reconcile   Print   ☐ Include Reconciled   Close

**3**   Calculate VAT

**4**   Printout?

**6**   Reconcile items?

**7**   Click Close

**Sage Line 50**

Show   Back   Forward   Print   Options

**Your VAT Return Checklist**

☐ Calculate your Sage Line 50 VAT Return.
☐ Print your VAT Return reports.
☐ Check your Sage Line 50 VAT Return.
☐ Back up your data.
☐ Reconcile your VAT transactions.
☐ Clear your VAT Control Accounts.
☐ Submit your VAT Return to the relevant tax authorities.

**Related Topics**
How your VAT Return is Calculated
Running the VAT Cash Accounting Scheme
Analysing the VAT Totals

## Tip

**The VAT Checklist in the Help pages will guide you through the whole job.**

**VAT Return Report**

VAT Return Type
☑ VAT Return
☐ Summary
☐ Detailed

Output
○ Printer
● Preview
○ File
○ E-mail

Run   Cancel

**5**   Print what and where?

# Summary

❑ The Audit Trail is the full record of all transactions that are still awaiting further processing.

❑ The Audut Trail should be cleared as part of the end of period routines to remove fully reconciled transactions.

❑ The end of month and end of year routines tidy up the system and calculate new end of period totals.

❑ The Trial Balance provides a summary of the state of the accounts – and if it doesn't balance, worry!

❑ The Profit and Loss account and Balance Sheet are based on a selected Chart of Accounts.

❑ The system will calculate the necessary figures for the VAT return and display them in the same layout as the VAT form.

# 9 Products

# New Products

If you will be using Product Invoices (see page 91), you need to enter the details of your products into the system. It's not difficult to do, but could prove to be a time-consuming chore if you handle a wide range of products.

The simplest way to set up a new product is through the New Wizard on the Products module.

The system can hold more a wider range of information than you may want to use. Don't overdo it. There's no point in entering useless information.

♦   The **Description**, **Code**, **Sale Price**, **Tax Code**, **Units** (i.e. are they sold in ones, dozens or hundreds) and **Nominal Code** are essential.

♦   If you use product **Categories**, or sales **Departments**, these should be selected.

♦   **Location**, **Commodity Code**, **Weight**, **Purchase A/C** code and (supplier's) **Part No**. can be omitted.

## Basic steps

1   In the Product window, click .

2   Enter a Description. Its first letters will be used to create the Code – edit this if necessary.

3   Enter the Location and other details if wanted.

4   Select the Category if used.

5   Enter the Sale Price, and change the Units, Tax code and Nominal account if the defaults do not suit.

6   Select the Department, if used.

7   Select the Supplier A/C and enter the Part No and Cost Price if wanted.

8   At the following panel you will be asked if you want to set an opening balance (see page 128)

9   Click [ Finish ].

**Product Record Wizard**                                              ✕

**Product Information**

**Entering your product description and unique code.**

To create a new product record you need to enter the product description and a unique reference.

Description  Bidet, white, 'Napoleon'

Code  BIDETNAPOLEO

Cancel                    Back    Next    Finish

2   Enter the Description and edit the Code as needed

**Product Record Wizard** ☒

Product Information

**Entering your Product details.**

Enter details about the product's category, location, commodity code and unit weight (where applicable).

Location    Aisle 2, Bay 4

Category    1 - Bathroom fittings ▾

Commodity code

Weight    0.00 ▦

Cancel          Back    Next    Finish

---

**3** Enter details if required

**4** Select the Category?

---

Tip ✓

**If details are not known when working on the Wizard, leave them out and enter them later by editing the product record (see next page).**

---

**Product Record Wizard** ☒

Product Information

**Entering your product sales details.**

Enter sales details of this new product record, i.e. selling price, department, units of sale etc.

Sale price    95.95 ▦     Department    1 - Plumpton ▾

Tax code    T 1 17.50 ▾     Unit of Sale    1

Nominal    4000 ▾     Item Type    Stock Item ▾
                                  Stock Item
                                  Non-Stock

Cancel          Back    Next    Finish

---

**6** Select a Department?

**7** Give the purchase details

---

...d Wizard ☒

Product Information

**Entering your product purchase details.**

Enter the purchase details of this new product record, i.e. Supplier account and Supplier part no.

Supplier A/C    KLENEWA ▾

Part No.

Cost Price    45.52 ▦

Cancel          Back    Next    Finish

---

**5** Set the Price, Units, Tax code and Nominal account

# The Products module

The Products module window is one of the less interactive parts of the system – which figures, as there is not a lot you can do with the products, except keep a track of them and use product information in the creation of invoices.

The tools in this window let you create new product records, edit old records, update stock levels and print the information.

Creating records was covered on the previous page. Let's see how to edit records, so that you can correct errors, add missing details and change prices.

## Basic steps

1   Select the record(s) you want to edit.

2   Click [Record].

3   Edit the record.

4   Click [Save].

5   Click [Next] if there are more records and repeat steps 3 and 4.

6   Click [Close].

New Product Wizard

View/edit selected records

Activity (see note)

Stock In/Out

Stock Take

Print reports

**Products**

| New | Record | Activity | In | Out | Stk Take | Reports |

**1  Select the record(s)**

**Products**   (All Records)

| Product Code | Description | Sales Price | Qty |
|---|---|---|---|
| BASINCERAMICROUNDPINK | Basin, ceramic, round, pink | 65.95 | 3.00 |
| BASINFREE | Basin, 'Freeflow'.Ceramic, Round, White | 87.50 | 5.00 |
| BATHENAMELWHITE | Bath,'Superior', Enamel, White | 145.00 | 4.00 |
| BATHPLASTICPINK | Bath, plastic, pink | 120.00 | 2.00 |
| BATHPLASTICWHITE | Bath, plastic, white | 99.95 | 2.00 |
| BATHPLUG | Bath plug | 1.15 | 12.00 |
| BIDETNAPOLEON | Bidet, white, 'Napoleon' | 95.95 | 2.00 |
| HANDRAIL400CM | Handrail, 400cm | 9.99 | 5.00 |

| Search | Swap | Clear | Delete | Print List | | Close |

**2  Click Record**

## Take note

The Activity button shows the same information that you get on the Activity panel of the record display.

## Tip

To select *all* the records, click Clear, then Swap.

**Product Record - Bath,'Superior', Enamel, White**

Details | Memo | Activity | Web |

**3** Edit the record

Product Code  BATHENAMELWHITE    Item Type  Stock Item
Description   Bath,'Superior', Enamel, White
Category      1 Bathroom fittings
Location                        Weight        0.00
Com. Code

Ordering
Cost Price        0.00

Stock levels can be recorded here or in the Stock Take dialog box (next page)

**Defaults**
Nominal Code  4000         Tax Code   T1 17.50
Supplier A/C  KLENEWAY     Part No.
Department    0

**Sales Price**
Price         145.00
Unit of Sale  1

**Status**
In Stock      5.00      OB

**Stock Take**
Date      10/07/2002
Quantity       5.00

Save | Discard | Delete | Back | Next | Print List | Close

**6** Click Close

**4** Click Save

**5** Go to the next

## Creating Product records while invoicing

If, while generating an invoice, you find that a product is not on the system, click the New button on the Products list.

### Tip

**After you save a record, the fields will be cleared of all except the default values. Don't let this worry you — your data is safe!**

**Invoice**

Details | Order Details | Footer Details | Payment Details |

Type    Invoice          Product Invoice
Format  Product    Inv.No.   <AutoNumber>
Date    18/07/2002    Order No
A/C           Item No.    No Items

| Product Code | Description | Qty | Price | Net | V.A.T. |
|---|---|---|---|---|---|

**Products**                          (All Records)

| Code | ▽ | Name |
|---|---|---|
| M | | Message Line |
| S1 | | Special Product Item, Tax chargeable |
| S2 | | Special Product Item, Tax zero rated |
| BASINCERAMICROUNDPI | Basin, ceramic, round, pink |
| BASINFREE | Basin, 'Freeflow',Ceramic, Round, White |
| BATHENAMELWHITE | Bath,'Superior', Enamel, White |
| BATHPLASTICPINK | Bath, plastic, pink |
| BATHPLASTICWHITE | Bath, plastic, white |

0.00    0.00
0.00    0.00
0.00

Search | New | OK | Cancel

Create a new Product record

Save | Discard | Print

Close

**127**

# Stock levels

The Product records can be used to keep track of stock levels. You can enter the quanitities in stock when first setting up a record or after a stock take. When goods are sold via invoices, the movements out are automatically marked on the product record. Deliveries, non-invoiced sales and other movements can be handled through the In and Out routines in the Product module.

## Opening balance

At the penultimate stage of the New Product Wizard, you will be asked if you want to enter an opening balance. If the numbers are known, this is a good time to do it.

## Stock movements

The Products module has three routines for recording changes:

 Adjustment in – deliveries and returns.

 Adjustment out – sales and losses.

 Updating the files after a manual stock take.

The dialog boxes are almost identical. The In dialog box also has a field to record the current cost, and the Stock Take has fields to record the actual number in stock and the adjustment.

---

## Take note

**In Accountant Plus and Financial Controller versions of the Sage systems you can get summaries of stock levels, items out of stock and on order, through the Task Manager.**

---

## Basic steps

❑ Opening balance

1 At the fifth screen of the New Wizard, select Yes, I wish to enter an opening balance.

2 Enter the Date, Quantity and Cost Price.

❑ Adjustments

3 Click .

4 Select the Product Code.

5 Set the Date.

6 Enter a Ref if required.

7 Enter the Qty (In/Out) or Actual (Stock Take).

8 When making an In adjustment, enter the Cost Price if it has changed.

9 Repeat steps 4 to 8 for other products.

10 Click Save then Close.

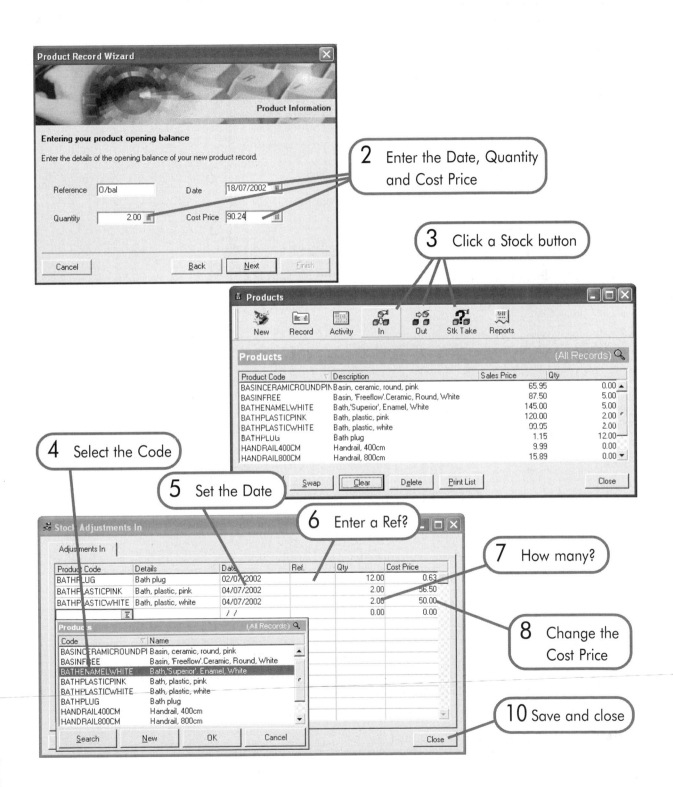

**2** Enter the Date, Quantity and Cost Price

**3** Click a Stock button

**4** Select the Code

**5** Set the Date

**6** Enter a Ref?

**7** How many?

**8** Change the Cost Price

**10** Save and close

# Summary

❑ Product records are produced through the New Product Wizard. Non-essential information can be omitted or added later.

❑ In the Products module you can create new product records, edit old records, update stock levels and print details of your products.

❑ Details can be edited at any time, simply select the records and click the Record button to start.

❑ Stock levels are updated as goods are sold through invoices, and can also be adjusted through the In, Out and Stock Take routines.

# 10 Help and support

# Help

Sage Accountant is a large system with very many features. Some of these you may never use, as they are not applicable to your business, others will be used only rarely, at year-ends or when particular problems arise. So, though you will soon be at ease with the routine chores – most of which should be covered in this book there will be times when you find yourself saying, 'How do I do this?' At times like this, turn to the Help pages.

To find information, you can browse through the **Contents**, or look it up in the **Index** or **Search** for it.

## Contents

The Contents panel offers the best approach when you are looking for Help with a module or operation. Here, the Help pages are organised into sections, with two or three levels of subdivisions. If the first page that you find does not tell you quite what you want to know, look for the links to related pages, and follow these up to find the answer.

◆ Look in the *Welcome* and *Setting up* sections for Help with the use of the software.

◆ Look in the *Accounts and Bookkeeping Procedures* section for Help with accounting concepts and techniques.

◆ Look in the *Glossary* for explanations of accounting or computing terms.

1 Open the Help menu and click Contents and Index.

*Or*

2 Click the Help button and select Contents and Index.

3 If necessary, click the Contents tab.

4 Click ◈ to open a section – repeat until you reach a page.

5 Click on words with a solid underline to jump to linked pages or to get a definition of the term.

6 Click the Back button to return to the previous Help page.

7 Close the Help window when you have done.

## Tip

**The Help window sits on top of all others. Minimise it when not in use if you want to refer to it again later.**

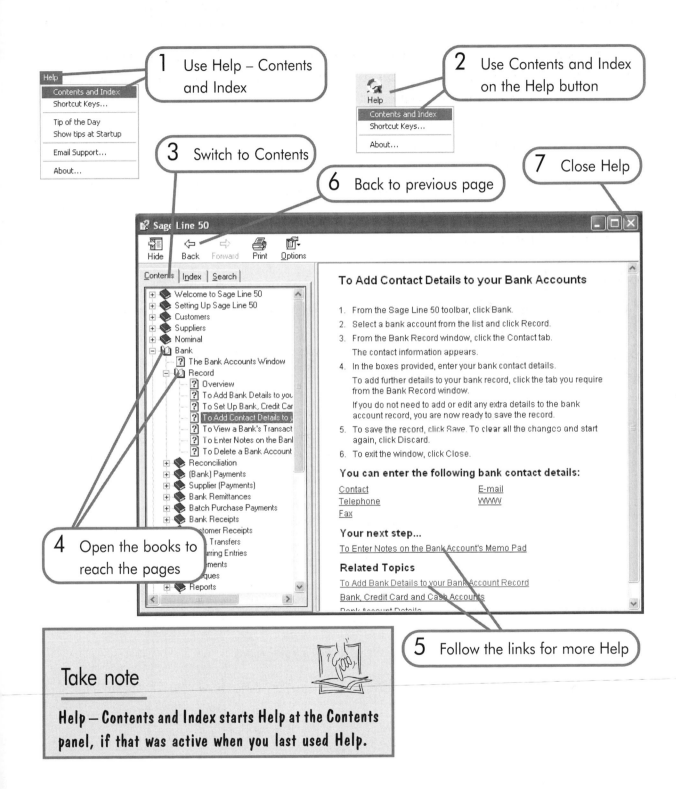

**1** Use Help – Contents and Index

**2** Use Contents and Index on the Help button

**3** Switch to Contents

**6** Back to previous page

**7** Close Help

**4** Open the books to reach the pages

**5** Follow the links for more Help

Help
Contents and Index
Shortcut Keys...
Tip of the Day
Show tips at Startup
Email Support...
About...

Help
Contents and Index
Shortcut Keys...
About...

**Sage Line 50**

Hide | Back | Forward | Print | Options

Contents | Index | Search

- Welcome to Sage Line 50
- Setting Up Sage Line 50
- Customers
- Suppliers
- Nominal
- Bank
    - [?] The Bank Accounts Window
    - Record
        - [?] Overview
        - [?] To Add Bank Details to you
        - [?] To Set Up Bank, Credit Car
        - [?] To Add Contact Details to y
        - [?] To View a Bank's Transact
        - [?] To Enter Notes on the Banl
        - [?] To Delete a Bank Account
    - Reconciliation
    - (Bank) Payments
    - Supplier (Payments)
    - Bank Remittances
    - Batch Purchase Payments
    - Bank Receipts
    - stomer Receipts
    - Transfers
    - urring Entries
    - ments
    - ques
    - Reports

**To Add Contact Details to your Bank Accounts**

1. From the Sage Line 50 toolbar, click Bank.
2. Select a bank account from the list and click Record.
3. From the Bank Record window, click the Contact tab.
   The contact information appears.
4. In the boxes provided, enter your bank contact details.
   To add further details to your bank record, click the tab you require from the Bank Record window.
   If you do not need to add or edit any extra details to the bank account record, you are now ready to save the record.
5. To save the record, click Save. To clear all the changes and start again, click Discard.
6. To exit the window, click Close.

**You can enter the following bank contact details:**

Contact                     E-mail
Telephone                   WWW
Fax

**Your next step...**

To Enter Notes on the Bank Account's Memo Pad

**Related Topics**

To Add Bank Details to your Bank Account Record
Bank, Credit Card and Cash Accounts
Bank Account Details

**Take note**

Help – Contents and Index starts Help at the Contents panel, if that was active when you last used Help.

# The Help Index

The Index contains nearly 2000 entries and sub-entries, in alphabetical order. You can scroll through to find an entry, but it is quicker to type in the first few letters of a word and jump to the relevant part of the Index. Most entries lead to a single page, but sometimes you will be offered a choice of pages from the same word.

If you were using the Index when you last shut down Help, the **Contents and Index** option will reopen Help at the Index.

1   Open the Help menu or click the Help button and select Contents and Index.

2   If necessary, click the Index tab.

3   Drag the slider to scroll through the index.

*Or*

4   Type the first few letters of the word to jump to the right part of the list.

5   Select an entry and click Display.

6   If the Topics Found panel opens to offer you a choice – select one and click Display.

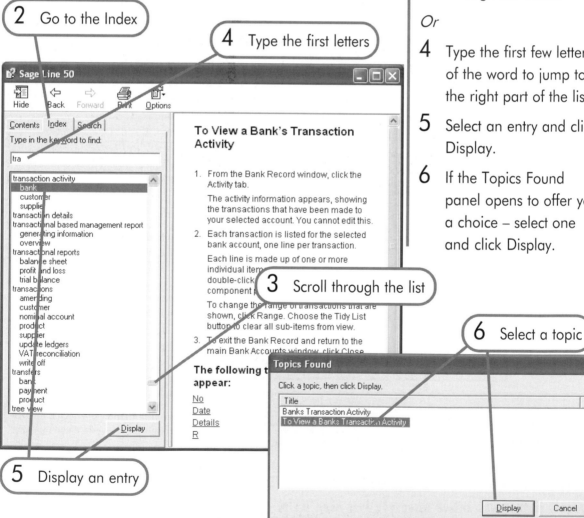

2   Go to the Index

4   Type the first letters

3   Scroll through the list

6   Select a topic

5   Display an entry

## Basic steps

1 Open the Help menu or click the Help button and select Contents and Index.

2 If necessary, click the Search tab.

3 Type one or more words to define the Help you need.

4 Select a topic from the bottom pane.

5 Click Display.

A Search hunts through the entire text of the Help system. It normally produces more results, as it will find every page containing a given word – not just the main ones on the topic. This can be useful as you can get a more thorough understanding of an issue by following up all the leads, but if all you want to do is find the meaning of a word, or learn how to do a particular job, it can take a bit longer to locate the relevant page.

If you were using the Search when you last shut down Help, the **Contents and Index** option reopens Help at the Search panel.

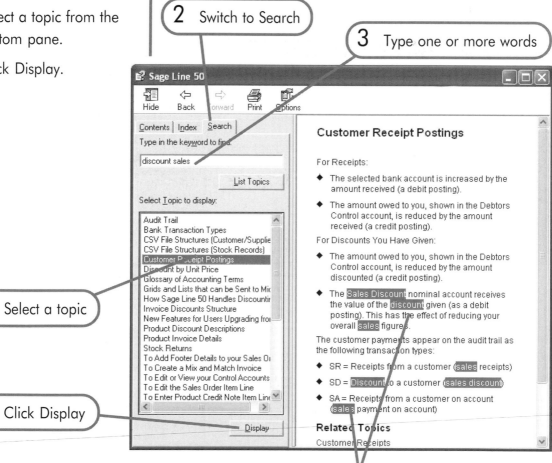

2 Switch to Search

3 Type one or more words

4 Select a topic

5 Click Display

The search words are highlighted

# Hide/Show

If you want to work on your accounts while keeping the Help window open, you may need to adjust your screen display so that you can see what you are doing.

Like any other window, the Help window can be resized and moved, but the most effective way to reduce its size is to hide the navigation panel. You can still go back through recently opened pages, or follow links from the current page, and if you need to get back into it, to find a different Help page, it is easily reopened.

**1** Click [🖳 Hide] to close the navigation panel.

**2** Work through your task, using the Help page for guidance as needed.

**3** Click [◀🖳 Show] if you need to open the navigation panel again.

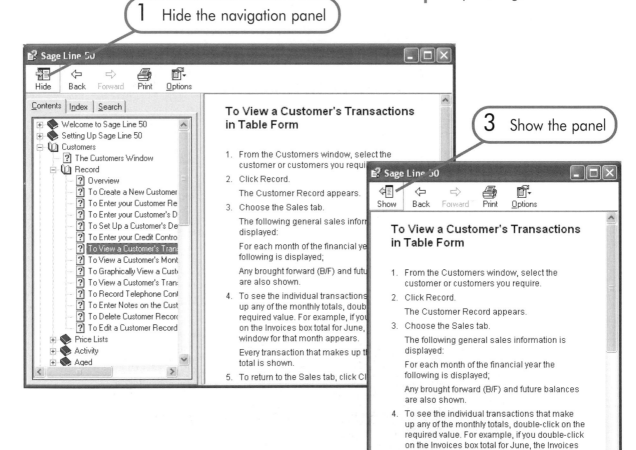

**1** Hide the navigation panel

**3** Show the panel

## Basic steps

1 Open the Help menu or click the Help button and select Shortcut Keys...

2 Make a note of any useful keys.

3 Click ⊠ to close the display.

# Shortcut keys

When the Sage system is active, the function keys [F1] to [F12] all have special purposes.

Check these out after you have been using the Sage system for a little while and see which ones it would be useful to learn. Though all functions can be accessed easily through the menus or toolbar buttons, when you are typing it is handy to be able to get to them directly from the keyboard.

You might like to note these in particular:

[F1]  Help – Contents and Index

[F2]  Runs the Windows Calculator

[F4]  Drops down the Code or A/C panel when invoicing, etc.

[F7] Insert a line into an invoice

[F8] Delete the current line of an invoice

[F9] Calculate the VAT from a net price.

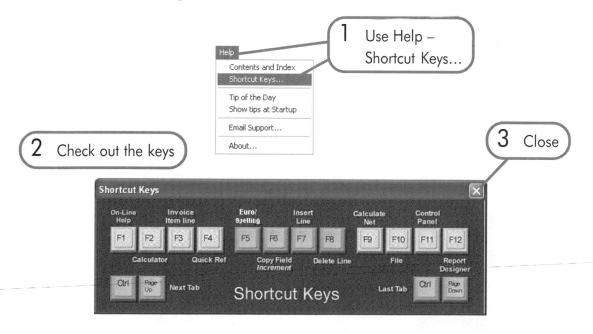

# Sage on the Web

The options on the sage.com button will fire up a browser and take you to Sage's Web site. The public part of the site contains mainly news and information about Sage and its products and services, though it also has some good articles on major topics.

Sage Cover subscribers have access to a section where you can get advice and assistance with the Sage systems and with accountancy and other aspects of business in general.

## Basic steps

1  Click **S** and select SageCover Home.

2  The latest articles are listed on the top page – browse to see what's there and click on a title to read the article.

3  Files, report layouts and 'Directors Briefings' documents can all be downloaded. Click to see the selection.

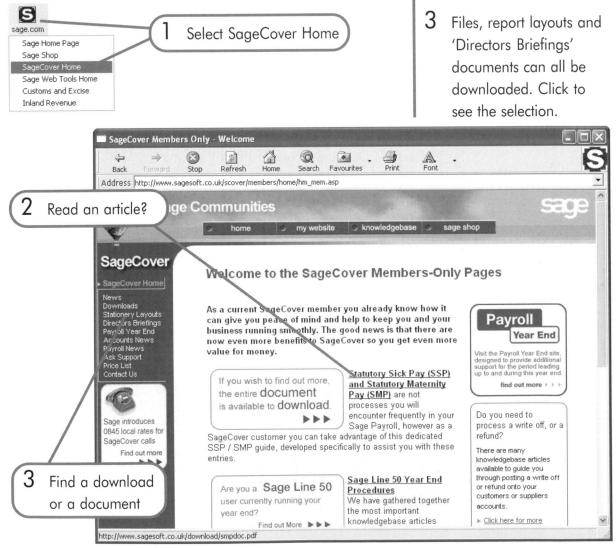

**4** Documents can be read on-line or downloaded. Click a title to start, then select read or save at the prompt.

**4** Select a document

Directors Briefings

Address http://www.sagesoft.co.uk/SCOVER/MEMBERS/DirectBrief/hm_dbrief.asp#tax

**SageCover**

SageCover Home

News
Downloads
Stationery Layouts
▸ Directors Briefings
Payroll Year End
Accounts News
Payroll News
Ask Support
Price List
Contact Us

Sage introduces
0845 local rates for
SageCover calls
Find out more
▶ ▶ ▶

Marketing
Corporate Finance
Finance
Insurance
Premises
Tax
Information Tech
Law
Strategy

## Directors Briefings

To run your business successfully, getting the right advice at the right time is critical. SageCover members have access to a range of business guides called Directors Briefings designed to give you that advice in an easy to understand format, when you need it.

To view or print these Directors Briefings, click on the relevant title below. You can then save this booklet to your computer as a PDF file. To view the booklet you need to have Adobe Acrobat Reader installed on your computer. If you don't already have a copy of Adobe Acrobat Reader, then click here. On the Adobe website click "Get Acrobat Reader" and follow the onscreen instructions.

**Human Resources Management**

| | |
|---|---|
| Everyday workplace policies | Using a consultant |
| Performance appraisals | Employment contracts |
| Leadership | Dismissing employees |
| Motivating employees | Redundancy |
| Managing change | Employment tribunals |
| Managing teleworkers | Maternity issues and SMP |
| Stress Management | Sickness issues and SSP |
| Discipline and grievance issues | Discrimination |
| Managing your time | Working time and the minimum wage |
| Investors in People | Remuneration |
| NVQs | Incentive pay |
| Using training effectively | Company pensions schemes |

## Take note

**Most documents are in PDF format. To read these you need Acrobat Reader. This can be downloaded — free of charge — from Adobe's Web site. Sage.com has links to Adobe, or you can go directly to www.adobe.com.**

# The Knowledgebase

One of the benefits of SageCover is access to the Sage Knowledgebase. This has FAQs (Frequently Asked Questions – and their answers), factsheets and other help on a wide range of topics. A simple search is all that is usually needed to locate the information that you need – just select a topic and enter keywords if you want to focus the search.

♦ If you can't find an answer in the Knowledgebase, go to Ask Support and e-mail your problem to their support staff.

1 Go to SageCover Home.
2 Click the Knowledgebase link.
3 Select your accounts system.
4 Define your search.
5 Click Search.
6 Select a Title – it will be displayed in a new browser window.

1 Go to SageCover

2 Click Knowledgebase

**Sage Knowledgebase**

Back  Forward  Stop  Refresh  Home  Search  Favourites  Print  Font  **S**

Address http://www.sagesoft.co.uk/Scover/members/CovKbase/search2.asp

**Sage Communities**

home | my website | knowledgebase | sage shop

**SageCover**

SageCover Home

News
Downloads
Stationery Layouts
Directors Briefings
Payroll Year End
Accounts News
Payroll News
Ask Support
Price List
Contact Us

Sage introduces
0845 local rates for

**Sage Knowledgebase**

4 Define your search

| | |
|---|---|
| Select a topic | Error Corrections |
| Select a document type | All |
| What's new in the last... | All |
| Select detail level of results | Simple ○ ● Detailed |
| Enter Keyword (optional) | Chart of Accounts |
| Begin search | Search  Reset |

Done

If you get too many results, select the document type and/or restrict it to newer documents

5 Click Search

**140**

Click Back in this browser window to return to the Search page

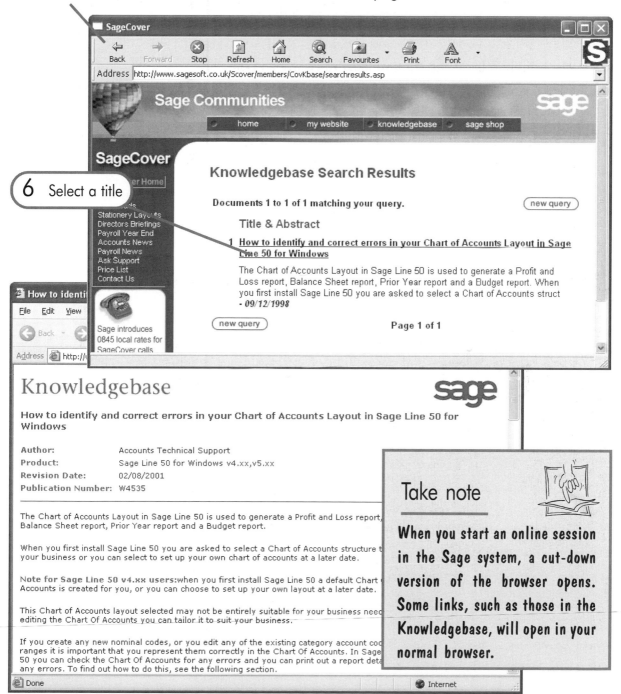

**6 Select a title**

# Summary

❑ There is plenty of Help available. You can browse through the Contents, or search for information in the Index or Search panels.

❑ If you want to refer to the Help window while working in the Sage window, you can hide its navigation panel so it takes up less space.

❑ The Sage system gives shortcuts to the function keys.

❑ You can start your Internet browser from within Instant Accounting. Any browser can be used, though Internet Explorer is recommended by Sage and is essential for interactive support.

❑ The Sage Web site has some useful information on its public pages and a great deal more in its SageCover section.

❑ The Knowledgebase is a valuable source of help on many aspects of Sage software and accountancy.

# Index